The Identity Advantage

Discovering Your God-Given Identity to Know
Who You Are and What You're Meant to Do

David Bostrom

Copyright © 2024 by David Bostrom

ALL RIGHTS RESERVED.

No part of this publication may be reproduced, stored in a retrieval system, or transmitted in any form whatsoever, electronic, or mechanical, including photocopying, recording, or otherwise, without the expressed written consent of the author, except as provided by USA copyright law.

Unless otherwise indicated, all Scripture quotations are taken from the New American Standard Bible®, Copyright © 1960, 1962, 1963, 1968, 1971, 1972, 1973, 1975, 1977, 1995 by The Lockman Foundation. Used by permission. (www.Lockman.org)

Cover and formatting by Diane Laffoon

Disclaimer: *The Identity Advantage* provides practical ideas concerning the application of the Bible to all of life. No guarantees are made that you will achieve any particular results from the Information presented.

Published by David Bostrom
MADE FOR DOMINION PRESS

www.madefordominion.com
info@madefordominion.com

ISBN: 979-8-9913201-0-8

Printed in the United States of America

Dedication

To the men who have helped me develop the ideas in this book through the lens of the Bible and real-world experience.

CONTENTS

INTRODUCTION 1

PART ONE: The Need for a Strong Identity 7

CHAPTER ONE: THE HOPE OF A NEW REALITY FOR MEN 9

CHAPTER TWO: WHY YOUR IDENTITY MATTERS 19

CHAPTER THREE: THE MAIN OBSTACLES TO YOUR TRUE IDENTITY 29

CHAPTER FOUR: BELIEVING AND RECEIVING IS THE KEY 41

CHAPTER FIVE: WHY FINDING YOUR IDENTITY CAN SEEM SO HARD 51

PART TWO: Your Identity's Foundation 61

CHAPTER SIX: THE BASIS OF YOUR IDENTITY 63

CHAPTER SEVEN: A BIBLICAL FRAMEWORK FOR LIVING 75

CHAPTER EIGHT: ESSENTIAL ELEMENTS OF A STRONG IDENTITY 87

PART THREE: Living Out Your God-Given Identity 99

CHAPTER NINE: PUTTING OFF THE OLD IDENTITY AND PUTTING ON THE NEW 101

CHAPTER TEN: LIVING OUT YOUR IDENTITY IN EVERYDAY LIFE 111

CHAPTER ELEVEN: MOVING INTO YOUR GOD-GIVEN PURPOSE 123

CONCLUSION: WHAT TO DO NEXT 135

ADDITIONAL RESOURCES 139

ABOUT THE AUTHOR 141

INTRODUCTION

Men are struggling these days. Many are in crisis. And at the heart of their struggle is knowing who they are and what they're supposed to do with their lives. That is, they are grappling for their identity and purpose. Compounding the problem, there are forces in our culture that make it difficult for men to know who they really are and what their lives are all about.

It's troubling so many men are wrestling with this issue. Understanding your identity and purpose is fundamental to life. And for centuries people didn't think much about discovering their identity—they just knew it, having received what was passed on to them. Yet the unfortunate reality today is that there's a lot of confusion about what it means to be a man. And if you are a man, you most likely recognize this problem in some way in your own life.

This book, *The Identity Advantage*, aims to guide men in discovering their God-given identity in today's world. And I've written it for three main reasons.

Why This Book

First, men today have lost their sense of identity.
If you ask the average man who he is, there's a good chance he'll have a hard time answering. He might say something about his vocation or role in his family, but he probably won't come up with anything that speaks to the core of who he really is–as a man. This lack of self-understanding is a serious problem. It's leaving men at a

major disadvantage, as it's hindering them from living out who God designed them to be. And it's affecting more than just men themselves.

Second, the cost of this loss of identity is high, both to men and society.
Men are the visionaries, builders and the protectors of our world. When they suffer, we all suffer. And due to their lack of clear identity, men today are suffering. They're hurting from aimlessness, fear, cynicism, depression, apathy, passivity, powerlessness, insignificance, addictions, hopelessness and more. And because men are plagued in these ways, we're missing out on all the good God intends for them to bring to the world.

Third, it's possible for any man to recover his true identity.
Many men today feel like they're a lost cause. They spend their days feeling down, drifting through life, unsure of where to turn. As a result, men of all ages are disengaging from life. But here's the good news. As a man realizes and embraces his true, God-given identity and begins to live it out, a transformation occurs. This process isn't difficult to enter into either–once he understands the identity God has for him. In other words, finding your identity doesn't have to be an abstract, years-long pursuit. You can discover it today. You just need to know where to look!

I've written *The Identity Advantage* to show you where to look.

This book isn't intended to be a literary masterpiece. Neither is it a comprehensive treatise on the subject of masculine identity. Rather, it's a straightforward guide for ordinary men who want to recover, reclaim and become established in their true, God-given identity as a man–in the most direct way possible.

I think most men will appreciate the plain approach of these pages. And though the book may never become a New York Times best

Introduction

seller, its message is pertinent to men of all ages. Since it speaks to issues at the core of their being, in any generation.

As this book gets underway, you may be wondering, "What can I expect from reading it?" That is a good question and here is my promise to you.

If you approach this book's message thoughtfully and with an open heart, you'll gain everything you need to understand your identity as a man. We'll clear away the rubble of misperceptions, cut through the clutter of modern culture, and get to the foundation of what it means to be a man. You'll also receive practical guidance on how to apply this personally.

And along with this, you will acquire a revived reason for living. Because by the time you finish the book, you'll see there's a close connection between your identity and your purpose. So once you recover your identity–and understand why it is what it is--your purpose will become clear.

To ensure you grasp this fully, we're going to cover three different areas.

Overview of Book

In part one we're going to consider why every man needs to be solid and secure in his identity.
A man who is unsure of his identity is like a boat without a rudder, adrift and at the mercy of external forces. In this state, he can't function as he's designed, and becomes a danger to himself and those around him. But once a man connects with his true, God-given identity, he can start sailing on an intentional course. This doesn't mean he won't face rough waters, but he'll be equipped to navigate them with a specific destination in view.

In part two we'll discuss the foundation of your identity.
Coming to terms with your identity may seem like a profound and elusive topic, but it doesn't have to be. As we'll discover, there's simplicity in understanding your identity and how to attain it. Once we uncover the true basis of your identity, it will provide the foundation you need to live the life God intends for you. And like the foundation of a house, once it's laid, it's there for good. So you can confidently build your life upon it.

Then in part three we'll look at what it takes to make the shift to your true identity, and what it means to live in it every day.
Your identity is at the core of how you function. So, it has significant implications for your daily life, influencing everything from your long-term aspirations to your daily choices and personal interactions. In this section, we'll explore the practical aspects of embracing your God-given identity, nurturing it, and putting it into practice in everyday situations. Whether you struggle with decision-making, standing up for your beliefs, overcoming temptations, or other challenges, this part of the book will demonstrate the advantages that come with having a clear and strong identity.

As we wrap up this introduction, I want to share a basic conviction of mine.

I believe it's absolutely essential for you, as a man, to be rock-solid in your identity. It's the only way you can know who God made you to be and fulfill the purpose for which He's given you life. You must be well-grounded here. I also believe coming to terms with your identity is something that can happen by the time you finish reading this book. And it's my hope you will have more than one eureka moment as you work your way through it.

Introduction

To do all I can to make sure this happens, I want to pass on the main point of the book right here at the start. It's what you might call the *master summary*, and it is this:

Your core identity is a gift from God, intricately woven into your very being. It's not something you need to earn or strive for–it's freely given to you. All you need to do is receive it by believing the One who created you. This journey may require shedding old beliefs and embracing new ones, but as you do, it will transform your life. It will encourage and strengthen you, providing a focused vision as you uncover the unique value you bring to the world while living in your God-given identity.

As we delve into *The Identity Advantage*, we'll unpack what all this means and how it applies to you.

But before getting into the material, I encourage you to download the free application guide that accompanies this book. It will help you apply the content effectively and gain the maximum benefit from it.

Access your own copy of **The Identity Advantage: Application Guide** here:

madefordominion.com/identity-book-extras/

May God use this material on recovering and establishing your God-given identity to transform your life, just as it has for many others.

PART ONE

The Need for a Strong Identity

CHAPTER ONE

THE HOPE OF A NEW REALITY FOR MEN

Everywhere you turn, people are talking about identity these days. Yet despite all the discussion, there's more confusion than clarity.

Sadly, we've lost touch with what ultimately defines us as individuals and people–which is what our identity is all about.

As one commentator describes it: "One of the big problems that we deal with in our society is identity. Everyone is always chattering about identity: racial identity, sexual identity, this identity, that identity. But no one knows who they are."

The confusion described here is impacting souls throughout our culture. Yet I believe it's particularly harmful when it comes to men. While women and children certainly have their own identity issues, I think the struggle men face in this area is especially detrimental. This is because the condition of men has a significant influence on society as a whole.

You see, men commonly cope with weak identities by disengaging from typical masculine responsibilities—as they isolate themselves with addictions, immerse themselves in hobbies or excess work, or withdraw emotionally. Unfortunately, when men use these methods as escapes, they neglect to harness their gifts for the betterment of the world around them.

If you are concerned about this, and want to become better established in your own true identity–so you can flourish and help address our current scenario–then keep reading. The pages that follow provide the identity-recovery plan we need.

I'd like to begin with some encouragement, hope and inspiration by exploring what it means to be strong in one's identity. So let's start by looking at ten attributes of men who are grounded in their God-given identity. Take note of the desirability of these qualities as you read them, and reflect on how incorporating them would change your own life.

Qualities of Men Grounded in Their God-Given Identity

1. **Self-Awareness:** With ongoing attention to their relationship with God, they continually grow in understanding of their identity as His sons, which empowers them to live by His grace.

2. **Godly Confidence:** Trusting God's faithful character, they approach life boldly, guided by His wisdom and providence.

3. **Resilience:** Grounded in God's love and care, they bounce back from adversity with unwavering faith, strength, and perseverance.

4. **Dependence on God:** They align their decisions with biblical truth, steadfast in their belief in God's sovereignty, even amidst resistance or other challenges.

5. **Emotional Intelligence:** They relate to others with understanding and compassion, keeping their emotional reactivity in check, as they're guided by the Spirit's wisdom.

6. **Integrity:** Committed to kingdom principles, they live by honesty, righteousness and moral courage–regardless of the circumstances.

7. **Teachability:** Open to correction and growth, they walk in humility and welcome new insights with grace and wisdom.

8. **Purpose:** Rooted in their identity as redeemed image-bearers, they pursue God's calling with vision and determination.

9. **Authenticity:** Secure in Christ, they prioritize faithfulness over appearances, living transparently in every situation.

10. **Empowered by the Spirit:** They rely on the Holy Spirit's guidance and strength, yielding to His leading in fulfilling their God-given purpose.

In addition to these beneficial qualities, here's another as a bonus...

Men who are grounded in their God-given identity are comfortable in their own skin as men. They are not swayed by the androgynous shift of our culture. Instead, they embrace the differences between men and women, and appreciate the unique strengths and glories of each sex.

These qualities may seem rare in today's world, and maybe even unattainable for men to embody in our current culture. We've become accustomed to living among men who are immobilized by a lack of masculine self-awareness. And as society fails to promote anything different, breaking out of the status quo can be challenging. However, it's essential to recognize that living in one's God-given identity is indeed possible for any man, completely transforming the quality of his existence.

The Hope of a Different Reality
Though the current state of affairs may be discouraging for many men, a brighter reality is within reach. Reflecting on those who have lived with strong identities in the past can inspire us to believe this.

Thankfully, history abounds with examples of men who understood their identity and operated within it to fulfill their God-given purpose. By recalling just a few of these individuals, we can broaden our perspective and envision a future where men are fully aware of their own God-given identities. And that vision should encompass you.

Let's explore a few of these examples, starting with the Bible. Scripture introduces us to various characters who possess a deep understanding of their identity. This self-awareness empowered them to live with vision, purpose, and a steadfast commitment to fulfilling God's plan.

Abraham stands out as a prime example. He was called by God and given the name 'Father of Nations' (Gen. 17:5). As this became the cornerstone of his identity, Abraham faithfully followed God wherever He led him. And Abraham's legacy endures, as all who have faith are his spiritual descendants.

Another example is David, renowned as a shepherd, poet, warrior and ultimately king of Israel. From his youth, David's identity was firmly rooted in God, making him capable of remarkable feats. And by living in this identity, he became regarded as a man after God's own heart (Acts 13:22).

The Apostle Paul, despite acknowledging himself as the chief of sinners (1 Timothy 1:15), understood that he was a new creation in Christ (2 Corinthians 5:17). This transformative realization superseded his past failures and bestowed on him a new identity. Empowered by this identity, Paul tirelessly carried out his life's mission throughout the Mediterranean world.

In addition to biblical examples, there are other notable instances of men functioning with strong identities…

Martin Luther grappled with a troubled conscience for years, but through an encounter with Scripture, his identity was transformed, making him a leader who gave birth to the Protestant Reformation.

John Newton made his living as the captain of a slave ship. Over time he came to see himself as a wretch, but by the grace of God his identity was changed and restored, and he's now known for his hymn, 'Amazing Grace.'

C.S. Lewis, following a journey from atheism to faith in Jesus Christ, underwent a significant transformation in his identity, ultimately becoming one of the greatest Christian apologists of the 20th century.

And from more recent days…

The television personality Mister Rogers, after becoming grounded in his identity, devoted himself to building a television platform to help the development of children.

David Green, the founder and CEO of Hobby Lobby, has remained steadfast in his Christian identity, which has influenced both the culture of his business and philanthropic endeavors, even amidst controversy.

And Ben Carson, who faced poverty and academic challenges, found strength in his faith, leading him to understand his identity, overcome obstacles, and ultimately become a world-renowned neurosurgeon.

I present these examples to offer insight into the transformative power of embracing one's God-given identity. And to encourage you to connect with and walk in your own God-given identity.

To further encourage you in this, I want to give you some present-day, unrecognized cases I'm directly acquainted with through my own work with men. This will be especially worthwhile if you are wondering if you can experience change and growth in your own identity.

A New Identity for Ordinary Men
Over the years I've had the privilege of being a part of the stories of men who have become transformed in their identities. It's always a thrill seeing these guys grow in an understanding of who they are, and then watch their lives change because of it. It's like watching a caterpillar become a butterfly. Here are a few cases I'll tell you about (with names altered to safeguard privacy).

Humbled Gary Gets a New Life
Gary had a fairly typical middle-class upbringing. He grew up in the Midwestern United States with parents who loved him. His family was a part of a church, but he never received any personal help with his spiritual development. While attending a major university, Gary spent some time dealing drugs. Yet after getting his act together, he graduated, took his first job, and soon got married. During these years Gary prided himself in 'being in control.' But his illusion of control shattered when his wife left him. So did his identity. Yet God used this time of suffering for good in Gary's heart, and this was the

start of a new beginning for him. Back in church, Gary found the grace He needed to reorient his life upon God and His principles. And he embarked on a journey of discovering what it means to be a man, which has transformed every part of His life. Today, Gary is remarried, a respected businessman, and leads other men in becoming who God intends them to be.

Struggling Joe Takes on Role as Family Leader
Joe had a tough childhood, marked by relentless work, a demanding father, and a household noisy with conflict. Early in his teens, Joe discovered alcohol as a way to cope. At eighteen, he enlisted in the Air Force to escape his family environment. During his service, Joe acquired valuable skills that led to lucrative business opportunities once his military days were over. Although Joe made good money, he continued to rely on alcohol to manage stress. Over the years, this dependency on alcohol led to several job losses and two divorces. Eventually, Joe became a Christian through the influence of friends. While the forgiveness he received brought great relief, he continued to struggle with alcohol. Through counseling, Joe confronted underlying issues and came to realize his past did not define him. Embracing his identity in Christ gave him strength to overcome his addiction. And now he enjoys using his skills and fulfilling a fatherly role in his family as he continues to grow in his faith.

Faithful Greg Finally Finds Fulfillment
Greg has been involved in his church throughout his life, serving God and others in various capacities. While this has always been rewarding for him, he has long felt a disconnect between his faith inside and outside of church. It's not that he forgets his faith outside of church. He just hasn't known how to apply it effectively and comprehensively. This disconnect has left him feeling unfulfilled, as if he's living a double life. In church, he adheres to a clear set of values, but at home and work these values don't seem to translate.

As a result, he often finds himself just trying to be a nice guy and nothing more. Everything changed when Greg began to understand his God-given identity. He now realizes God created him for a unique purpose, and he is meant to use his gifts and opportunities to build God's kingdom—not just in church, but in every area of his life. This newfound understanding has led Greg to apply his faith to all his interests, bringing him fulfillment and positively impacting those around him."

Homeschooled Joshua Discovers His Niche

Joshua received most of his education via homeschooling within his family, but for his junior and senior years he attended a private Christian school. Overall, his educational journey was quite positive, and he was known as a sharp, likable young man with a bright future. Yet deep down Joshua lacked confidence, and this made it difficult for him to commit himself in any direction–whether it be college or a vocation. So he bounced around from job to job without enthusiasm or purpose. After a few years of this, Joshua got frustrated and started investigating what it means to be a man. He ended up following a number of online influencers in what's known as the manosphere, but eventually concluded that though these leaders provided some helpful ideas about masculinity, they never got to the core of what it is to be a man. One day a friend introduced Joshua to our ministry, and he began to understand the biblical basis for his identity. This provided Joshua with new motivation and a clear direction for his life, which included a well-suited career path.

These stories demonstrate that when a man understands his true identity, it can completely transform his direction, purpose and level of confidence. These are just ordinary guys, but what sets them apart is their willingness to look at themselves honestly, acknowledge what they've been missing, and align with the truths they are learning. By doing this, they've become new men.

A New Reality for You

I don't know your history or the circumstances you are facing today, nor do I know how these are affecting your sense of identity. But I am confident your life can be transformed by establishing your identity on the right foundation.

It doesn't matter if you're...

- figuring out what's next for you
- feeling the squeeze from expectations and responsibilities
- recovering from a business, marriage, or moral failing
- seeking to break loose from from an addictive behavior
- wondering how to best use your experience and gifts
- feeling like you've wasted too much of your life for it to make a difference now
- or trying to navigate the many voices about identity in our culture

Whatever your situation, there is hope for you. It is possible for you to experience a whole new reality as you come to understand the identity God intends for you. And in this book I will outline the obstacles to avoid and principles to apply as you seek to recover your God-given identity.

This resource may provide just what you need to address some unresolved foundational life issues once and for all. Simply keep reading to see how the framework I'll describe applies to your life.

It's definitely worth finding out too. There's nothing like starting each day knowing who you are and what you're made to do with your life. Your focus increases. Temptations lose their appeal. And you see yourself functioning within God's larger plan for humanity.

In short, you become a man on a mission. What can be a better way to live than that?

Our current culture may make it seem impossible for a man to find and live in his true identity. But there is plenty of reason for hope. Continue reading to find out why. Reclaiming your God-given identity is attainable for you.

Breakthrough Insight:
Though there are plenty of people confused about who they are these days, there's a well-worn path made by men who have found their God-given identity. There's no reason you can't follow this same path.

CHAPTER TWO

WHY YOUR IDENTITY MATTERS

Most men I know want their lives to count for something. They hope to make a contribution and have a positive impact on their world. I assume this is true for you. But it's difficult for men to accomplish this in keeping with God's design if they are unclear about their true identity. And this has a significant cost for all of us.

The High Cost of Weak Identities Among Men

Today's widespread identity crisis among men extends beyond middle-aged individuals grappling with their unfulfilled youthful aspirations. It affects men of all ages who struggle to understand the purpose of their lives.

Consider this: If you ask a group of men who they are and most respond with a blank stare, it's clear there's a problem. It constitutes a crisis, as this lack of self-awareness will inevitably have negative effects wherever men exert influence.

This scenario is most costly to men themselves.
This isn't hard to see. If you don't know your identity–or you spend years trying to figure it out–much of your life can be squandered. Your talents remain untapped, opportunities pass by, and potential benefits go unrealized by others.

Peter, for example, was a gifted young man who wasn't afraid of work. Yet because he lacked a clear identity, he didn't know where to devote his attention and energy. So he ended up spending hours a day playing video games. Upon discovering his God-given identity, this changed. He gained a fresh vision for his life and began pursuing it diligently.

Men with weak identities also incur costs for their families.
This often takes place as a man fails to be present at home—not just physically, but emotionally. When a man doesn't know who he is or fails to grasp the weightiness of his life, he tends to live in his thoughts. In this state, he may be physically present but emotionally distant from his family. He may struggle to listen attentively, engage in family events, or recognize the influence of his actions. This lack of involvement can negatively affect his wife and children, giving the impression that he doesn't care, despite his genuine concern.

When men collectively suffer from weak identities, entire communities suffer.
Men must understand that they are created to provide vision, lead, develop, and protect. This is part of their identity. If they fail to understand this, they won't take sufficient notice of their surroundings and engage accordingly. Over time, this neglect leads communities to degrade and break down– spiritually, economically and socially. And the root cause often lies in men not embracing their true identity.

As this condition persists, entire cultures risk losing their identity. Cultures and civilizations also have distinct identities. When a civilization abandons its history and core beliefs, it loses its sense of self, direction, and resilience. Such societies forget why they exist and, without a spiritual awakening, may eventually self-destruct.

Your Identity is More Than an Abstract Theory

From the above, it's evident that understanding your identity goes beyond theory; it influences how you navigate your life and impacts all who are around you. This realization is what captured my attention and sparked my interest in this topic of identity. I'd like to share my story with you, as it illustrates how crucial it is to solidify your own identity.

Years ago, I served as a pastor and church planter. I was devoted to this work and found great enjoyment in it. I used my gifts in an area where I believed God had called me, helping people address significant life issues and fulfilling what I thought to be an important part in extending God's kingdom.

But shortly after crossing the 20 year mark, a change occurred. My family and I hit a wall, experiencing burnout. My wife also was dealing with some serious health problems that demanded our attention. This situation placed me in unfamiliar territory as a husband, father, and church leader. And I had to figure out how to balance the demands of my calling with the needs of my family.

After much prayer and soul-searching, I made the difficult decision to step down from my position as a pastor, believing it was the most responsible choice for my family and church. It was a painful experience, as it felt like something I loved was being taken away from me–and it wasn't part of my career plan! I faced anxiety about the future, too. Yet through it all, God used these events for good, revealing important truths to me, especially how tightly my identity had been intertwined with my role as a pastor.

Of course, many men find their identity in their work. There's an aspect of this that's good, healthy and necessary. God gifts, prepares, and calls men to serve the world through different vocations, and this is an integral part of their identity. Yet centering your identity here can make work an idol that totally defines you. This can lead to not only neglecting other crucial areas of life, but also missing the ultimate source of your identity.

Pastors can be especially vulnerable to this. After all, they're always doing 'God's work.' People look up to them–for the most part--and they're accustomed to having others listen to them for guidance. Being in this position can inflate a man's self-importance. And if he's not careful, he can hitch his entire identity here.

Not all pastors fall prey to this, but it's an occupational hazard, and it affected me. So when I was no longer a pastor, my identity was shaken. I wondered "Who am I?" For a while I didn't know the answer. Which made for a rough season–for me and those close to me—as I figured out who I was and what God had in store for me.

This set me on a hunt for my identity and its source. It was a time filled with discoveries, and in the process, I came upon a biblical framework that reshaped my understanding of who I am. This framework can likewise provide clarity for any man seeking to discover his identity from God's perspective—including you.

Realizing this framework was a eureka moment for me, as it completely transformed my self-understanding. And it led to five changes that continue to shape my life every day. I want to share these because they await any man who finds his own God-given identity.

First, having this new foundation for my identity gave me a far greater awareness of God's goodness and grace.
I lived most of my life as though my identity was something to attain on my own. So I carried a lot of self-imposed pressure to perform and become somebody others would affirm. But once I came to see God's design for my identity, I realized how good and gracious He is. And I came to rest in the truth that my core identity is not found in what I do or what people say about me, but in who He made me to be.

A second result of this new identity is that it liberated me from tying who I am too closely to my position or achievements.
Achieving and advancing in life are good things. God has wired men for it, but our core identity runs deeper than any accomplishment or title. When you understand this, it frees you up to live more in line with your true identity. And it actually makes you more effective in the places God calls you to serve.

A third benefit of coming to terms with my identity is that it's brought a renewed and better understanding of God's purpose for my life.
Specifically, I came to realize God's purpose for me is far greater than I had previously understood. I used to see my purpose mainly in terms of fulfilling my vocation and providing for my family. Now, informed by my God-given identity, I recognize the significance of everything I do within God's kingdom.

Fourth, discovering where my identity really comes from has made me grateful for my unique place in God's kingdom.
When I resigned from serving as a pastor, I wondered if I'd find much meaning in whatever I did next. Yet after understanding my identity in a more biblical way, I was able to see my part in God's story is still unfolding. He isn't finished with me. He just has a new assignment, where I can use my experience and gifts for His kingdom better than I envisioned.

Finally, one more benefit of this new understanding of my identity is that I have a more secure foundation moving forward in life.
I used to be pretty reactive to circumstances around me, often overly concerned about how others might view me. Now, I'm less fearful and more capable of pivoting and adapting as situations evolve. This change, without a doubt, stems from God opening my heart to understand where my true identity lies.

What I've described here is a real security-booster for any man. It makes him less threatened by whatever comes his way and more in tune to God's unfolding story in his life. This can definitely become something you experience for yourself. But before getting deeper into how, I want to point out an important aspect of my story.

The Value of Changes and Transitions
It wasn't until I found myself in a period of transition that the truth about my identity became apparent. This is often how it unfolds. God frequently uses challenging life-changes to expose our vulnerabilities and illuminate reality. This was my experience. What I saw was unsettling, but necessary. Because it opened my eyes to the truth I needed a better, more enduring source for my identity.

I mention this because transitions are inevitable in life, and they often challenge our sense of identity. Changes compel us to confront who we really are. This is why transitions can be difficult and why we sometimes try to avoid them. Yet transitions can lead us into seasons of necessary growth. But we'll only perceive them this way if we're open to a new foundation for our identity.

To see how this comes into play, let's consider the kind of transitions that tend to occur in the different quarters of a man's life. Doing so will help reveal why finding and staying rooted in your true identity always matters. I encourage you to apply what I describe here to your own situation.

First Quarter (zero to 24 years of age)
As a young man reaches the end of his first quarter, he's learning, exploring and gaining experience. He's also discovering what he likes and is good at. During this time there can be pressure from the expectations of others, creating anxiety and making it difficult to make major life decisions. Yet when a young man has a well-

grounded identity, it protects him from excessive outside influence. And it frees him to discern a sense of calling for himself, so he can consider which options before him best line up with who he is.

John, a recent college grad, excelled in school and had several promising job opportunities to choose from. Despite knowing his parents would support any decision he made, he felt anxious about his friends' opinions. This inner conflict puzzled him until he gained clarity about his true identity. Once he did, his mind calmed, and the path forward became clear.

Second Quarter (zero to 25-45 years of age)

During this phase, men typically focus on honing their skills, seeking further training or mentoring, and expanding their professional network. It's also a period when many men encounter increasing family demands, which can lead them to feel pulled in multiple directions. Amidst these competing demands, maintaining clarity about one's identity can be challenging. Yet remaining aware of his true identity is crucial for a man to navigate this season faithfully.

Ben wrestled with a significant portion of this phase. He was plagued by doubts—doubts about whether he was in the right job, uncertainties regarding his relationship with his wife, and even questioning whether God cared about him. But his uncertainties faded after he anchored himself in the true source of his identity. And this transformation made him a more decisive and proactive man.

Third Quarter (46-64 years of age)

At this stage, the demands on most men intensify. There are expectations to excel across various life domains–requiring energy, consistency, wisdom and selflessness. It can be daunting for men to focus under this pressure, leading to frustration as they perceive a gap between their aspirations and reality, potentially triggering an identity crisis. Yet those rooted in their God-given identity are able to thrive during this period, as they maintain their purpose, integrity, and optimism despite the challenges they face.

Lucas was remarkable to those who knew him well, juggling his own business, community responsibilities, and an active family life. Despite his full schedule, Lucas never appeared frazzled. When asked about his secret, he attributes it to maintaining perspective. When pressed further, he explains that he works diligently to stay aware of his identity from God's perspective, which helps him keep his focus in the right place.

Fourth Quarter (65 years of age and beyond)
In this last phase, a man will ordinarily reflect on his accomplishments and think about his legacy. Many men may also experience a sense of uselessness. And with this comes a temptation to sit on the sidelines and watch life go by, often in self-pity. But when a man at this stage is sure about his identity, there's an ability to adapt and enter new areas of service. Which can be incredibly fruitful as he brings his experience to bear in brand new contexts.

Chuck retired from a fulfilling career and was surrounded by grandchildren. Despite this, he felt restless. With unused abilities and ample time on his hands, golfing and lunching with friends couldn't fill the void, and he began to feel depressed. But after understanding more about his identity and how to live it out, Chuck recognized the opportunity to explore long-deferred interests and discover new ways to serve others. This revitalized him and brought a renewed purpose to his retirement.

Everyone experiences these phases in one form or another, and navigating them successfully largely depends on how deeply rooted we are in our God-given identity.

It's important to remember too... There are countless other changes that may take place at any stage of life. There are changes in jobs, bosses or businesses. Changes in where you live. Changes in health, relationships, responsibilities. And changes in your views on any of umpteen issues. All of which require adjustments or transitions in some form. Whether you face these changes with anxiety and confusion or hope and direction will depend on where you're at with your identity.

This applies to small, everyday issues too. For example, how you handle unsettling words from another person will hinge on the strength of your identity, and will lead you to respond either constructively or destructively. So coming to terms with who you really are is of great practical significance in your everyday dealings.

I've taken time to elaborate on the transitions we face because changes are a big, ongoing part of life. And whether you manage their highs and lows well or not is connected to the condition of your identity. So I hope this encourages you as we proceed–especially if you are currently in a major transition.

As we wind down this chapter, you may be thinking, "I'm just an ordinary guy–a Christian striving to live by faith in Jesus. Do I really need to go any deeper than that?" To you I'd say: I understand your perspective and don't want to overcomplicate the simplicity of faith. But in God's kingdom, there is no such thing as an ordinary guy. Each of us has a distinct and significant mission to fulfill in our own corner of the world, within our unique time in history. And to carry out that mission effectively, it's crucial to be firmly grounded in your identity.

Breakthrough Insight:
No matter who you are or where you're at in life, your identity matters. How you see yourself affects not only your own life, but your family and community as a whole. This makes knowing who you are essential to fulfilling the purpose God has for you as a man in His kingdom, through all the changes and transitions life brings.

CHAPTER THREE

THE MAIN OBSTACLES TO YOUR TRUE IDENTITY

Coming to know your true, God-given identity may seem hard to accomplish–especially in our current culture. But it's actually quite a straightforward matter when approached the right way, as we'll see later. Yet there are a few obstacles to dodge, and I'd like to take a look at the three biggest hurdles here.

Obstacle #1: Ignoring the Issue of Your Identity
As talk about identity gains momentum in our society, you're likely becoming more aware of the topic. You may even have questions about it too–especially as it relates to you as a man. Despite this, you might not feel compelled to give the subject much thought, so you mostly ignore it. And there may be several reasons why.

First, you're busy. The demands of everyday life consumes your time and energy, leaving little room for introspection. In the midst of your obligations, contemplating profound questions about who you are may not be at the forefront of your mind. So you occupy yourself with the business of living, and leave any identity questions aside. I get it. But consider this… taking time to address questions about your identity might be just what you need to assure you are hustling in the right direction, and for the right reasons.

Also, pondering your identity may seem abstract and complex to you. Life is complicated enough, so the idea of delving into this topic might seem overwhelming. With all the different views of identity circulating today, you may wonder, "Where do I even begin?" So you decide it's easiest not to start at all. But don't let the appearance of difficulty dissuade you from coming to terms with the basis of your identity. As mentioned before, this is completely within reach for anyone.

And finally, you might want to ignore the identity issue because it's a highly charged one. You may prefer to avoid the controversy this topic could bring. So, going with the flow and accepting the status quo may seem like the best course for you–even if it means missing out on the chance to solidify your own personal identity.

If any of this describes you, I'd challenge you to consider something important…

Understanding your identity is crucial to every facet of life. And to fulfill your God-given purpose, you must have a clear sense of self. So I urge you to give this topic some careful thought. This book will help you by establishing the biblical foundation of your identity and exploring its practical implications in the real world.

Having considered this first obstacle to discovering your God-given identity, let's move on to the second…

Obstacle #2: Getting Your Identity from Elements of Your Life Story
Each of us has a narrative that shapes our lives. Embedded within these narratives are various experiences that mold the way we see ourselves. While these experiences undoubtedly influence us, they do not define the essence of who we are.

Yet it's extremely common for people to find their identity in certain aspects of their story. In what follows, I want to share some common story elements that people tend to use as the basis of their identity. By recognizing these patterns, you may gain insight into your own story and its influence on your sense of self.

1) School
Some people have strong identity attachments to their school. Imagine someone who went to a prestigious Ivy League university. It's easy to see this person getting his identity from this connection, even making sure you know it is part of his resume. But now think of somebody who did not attend a well-known school, or any college at all. This may affect his identity as well, but in an adverse way.

2) Association with a club, team or organization
Guys often find a sense of identity in groups they are associated with. This isn't necessarily a bad thing. God made us social creatures, and men need a band of brothers to function at their best. But if a man clings to a sports team, club membership or political affiliation as a substantial part of his selfhood, then he's likely missing where his core identity lies.

3) Money and possessions
Money and possessions can be a great blessing from God, but they also can be a trap if one's identity depends on them. There are many souls who chase riches as a way to make a name–or identity–for themselves. Though common, this is a dangerous way to find your sense of self, since material wealth is fleeting.

4) Appearance
Our culture places a lot of importance on appearance. And by appearance, I'm not only referring to physical attractiveness, but also appearing popular, successful, or as though you're living 'the

good life.' All this can make for a shallow sense of identity. And an emphasis on image can improperly inflate or diminish someone's sense of self.

5) Fitness

Some people build their entire identity around the fact they're in good shape. Their physical prowess is what most defines who they are. Certainly, there's a place for men to pursue strength, since it's an attribute of masculinity, but be careful of fixing your identity here. We age, bodies deteriorate, injuries occur… and when they do, you don't want your identity based on how much you can lift or how ripped you are.

The next elements might seem a little unconventional at first glance. You may not immediately recognize them as places where people anchor their identity. But stay with me, and I believe you'll come to see that these are indeed areas where some individuals find their identity in today's world.

6) Afflictions

Through the years I've known people who have had a disease or a handicap define who they were. Their identity was rooted in being a cancer patient or paraplegic, for example. But I've also known those with major conditions that did not dominate their identity. Their affliction was part of their story, but it didn't set the terms of who they were as people. There was more to them than their affliction.

7) Sins

Similarly, there are those who have their identities set by sinful habits or addictions. Today, it's common for men who have struggled with bad tempers, alcohol addiction, or compulsive sexual habits to have their sense of self molded by their history with these behaviors. These men can feel trapped by the negative influence of their past or present battles. Yet it's possible for them to enjoy the freedom a new identity brings, as we'll explore later on.

8) Race
Race has affected how people view themselves for centuries, especially among minority populations. And in our day, race has become the dominant identity factor for some people groups, marking the rise of a new tribalism. A lot of this is driven by politics. But wherever it occurs it's unfortunate, because as the Bible teaches, race is not the basis for one's identity (Gal. 3:28).

9) Gender
Gender is also a big issue today. Yet, biblically speaking, it also is not the primary locus of one's identity. In God's providence, He creates some members of mankind male and some female, each with different attributes and functions. But in the end, your value doesn't come from being either a man or a woman.

10) Victimhood
Many people believe life has mistreated or cheated them. This leads them to see themselves as disadvantaged and adopt the identity of a victim. This victim mentality permeates every aspect of their self-perception, and is often accompanied by a sense of entitlement to compensate for perceived losses. Unfortunately, those who identify as victims miss out on discovering their true identity and the benefits that come with it.

All these items are what I call 'story elements' in that they are common components of the life story someone may have. Keep in mind, the elements any of us have in our story come from the hand of God, as He works out His plan for our lives. Without a doubt, these elements shape the direction of our lives and affect who we become, but they do not form the fundamental essence of who we are.

Put another way… the pieces of your story are peripheral elements when it comes to your identity. Not in the sense they're unimportant, but that they're outside of what matters most. What really makes the difference is your true, core God-given identity–which is always stable, regardless of the nature of your story. And, you will be strongest and most fruitful when your life is grounded in this identity, not in the peripheral elements of your life narrative.

Obstacle #3: Confusing Your Identity with Your Roles
One last obstacle to deal with is assuming that your identity comes mainly from your roles. We all have roles to fill, and these roles are a healthy and important aspect of carrying out God's purpose for our lives. But sometimes these roles end up carrying too much weight regarding our identity.

I've saved this obstacle for last because it can be a little tricky to understand. The reason is that our roles actually do have a part to play in our identity. We just need to keep them from becoming the totality of who we are. I'll show you what I mean as we consider some roles you can relate to as a man.

Roles within the Family
If you are a man, there are certain roles you are surely familiar with. At a minimum, you are a son. You are some couple's male child. But you may also be a brother, husband, and father. Any or all of these relations can serve to fill out aspects of your identity. We know this because the Bible sees these relations as identity factors.

Jesus, for example, is portrayed as a son (of earthly parents and God the Father), a husband (to the church) and a brother (to both earthly and spiritual brethren). When the Bible speaks of Jesus this way, it's making certain identity statements about Him—He is a son, husband, and brother. And, as God-incarnate, He shows how to flesh out these roles as a reflection of the ideal masculine identity. So, when we possess these roles, and take on the identity aspects related to them, we learn how to function in them by looking to Him.

Yet here is where it gets a little tricky. As important as these roles are as real, legitimate aspects of a man's identity, the essence of who a man is runs deeper and is more permanent. And this has a lot of practical importance.

Consider, for example, if a man:

- Becomes a widow or gets divorced
- Falls short as a husband or father
- Or is single and doesn't have children

Is this man doomed to a deficient identity?

Not at all, since these relations aren't the totality of who he is. And a more firm basis of identity awaits him, as we'll see as this book continues.

Roles Related to Gifts, Skills and Work
God gives men different abilities and callings, and these too serve as a reflection of their identity. In the Bible, there's a character named Bezalel who was gifted as a craftsman (Ex. 31:1-6). He was known for this, and his gift and calling are a part of who he was.

In a similar way, we have people with particular gifts and callings that reflect their identity today. You know people who are good with numbers, adept at leading or managing people, able to communicate well, skilled in technology, creating things, giving counsel, etc. As these folks are known for doing their thing, and deploy their gifts and callings in serving others, it conveys a part of their identity.

This includes those with unique or obscure talents. For example, a beekeeper might not only possess skills to preserve the bee population, but also use his honey harvest to promote health and wellness or support local charities. If you have what you might consider a unique ability, consider how you can best use it to fulfill God's design for you, as doing so is a reflection of your identity.

When it comes to roles related to skills, gifts and work, there are a few cautions in order.

If you are especially gifted, you will likely make certain achievements and be rewarded for it. If so, praise God. He wired men to achieve and we glorify Him when we do so. Yet be careful not to let your achievements become the foundation of your identity. And, of course, beware of pride too. The day is coming when people won't remember your accomplishments, so it makes sense not to have your identity rooted in them today.

If you consider yourself average, with more modest accomplishments, you need to be careful in a different way. You must guard yourself against discouragement, and from striving to achieve certain goals in order to become somebody. You already are somebody. And when your identity is properly grounded, you can stay content and faithful no matter what achievements you attain or recognition you receive.

And this really applies universally… Remember, things change. Gifts don't always shine like they used to. Attention you get from others wanes. And jobs come and go. Situations like these–which happen all the time–highlight the need for our identity to be founded upon something more than a role we fill or skill we use for a fleeting period of time.

Roles within Society

There's one last area I'll mention here as it pertains to confusing roles with identities. This has to do with different roles a man may have in society.

One example of this would be a church leader. The Bible tells us for a man to aspire to be a church leader is a fine thing (1 Tim. 3:1). And serving in this position can be a positive part of a man's identity, as he functions as an undershepherd of Jesus Christ. This role can also constructively shape a man's identity as he considers how to conduct himself in the role. But there are dangers here too, especially if a man finds his identity more in his position as a church leader than in his relationship with God. In this case, too, pride can make a man lax in spiritual discipline, affecting both his personal life and quality of leadership.

Another role in society to consider is that of a citizen. Today, in our global society, the whole idea of citizenship is being undermined and undervalued. But the God who sets boundaries and establishes nations still has a place for citizens. Consequently, citizenship has a part in the shaping of our identities. This should lead us to live as caring and trustworthy neighbors who love our country and seek its best interests. And we are able to accomplish this best when we find our primary citizenship and identity with God and His kingdom.

Related to the role of a citizen is that of a veteran. We often regard veterans as the heroes of society, because of their willingness to sacrifice and even die for their country. In keeping with a man's protective role, this is noble and worthy of honor. And so is maintaining a warrior spirit as a man. Yet for some men, military service lives on as the main part of their identity. They may show this in the clothes they wear, signs in their yard, bumper stickers on their car, etc. There's no problem with this as a show of solidarity. But caution is in order for anyone inclined to fix his identity more in being a veteran of his nation's military than serving as a soldier of Christ Jesus.

> **Pause to Apply:** With the obstacles mentioned above in mind, where are you most inclined to find your identity?

Take Note of Your Tendencies

I hope this chapter has helped you see the many places we may tend to find our identity. And I encourage you to take note of your own tendencies in this regard. We all possess a need to have our identity grounded somewhere. Yet we must be wary of grounding it in those aspects of our lives that are temporary. These aspects certainly have their place in the various ways we fulfill God's call to rule and cultivate the earth, but they also can get in the way of finding our God-given identity.

Keep in mind too: finding your identity involves a kind of spiritual warfare. The enemy of your soul wants you to locate your identity somewhere other than where God intends. He knows this will diminish your fruitfulness in His kingdom and lead you to miss your true purpose. So be aware of these obstacles.

If you stay conscious of these obstacles, they become easier to overcome. And by finding your identity where God intends, every element of your story and every role you fill can have its place as God uses you to further His purpose throughout your life.

Breakthrough Insight:

Be aware of the various obstacles that can keep you from adopting your true, God-given identity. Recognizing and overcoming those that affect you most is a necessary part of knowing who you are.

CHAPTER FOUR

BELIEVING AND RECEIVING IS THE KEY

In all my years working with men, one of the things that stands out is that those who excel in their different domains have confidence. They live 'with faith' and believe the outcomes of their lives will be favorable–no matter what challenges are before them. And I've observed this trait in men across all kinds of callings and situations.

A natural question this raises is, where do such men get their confidence? And how can any man get more of it for himself?

There are a couple ways to look at this.

The first observation is that many factors contribute to a man's confidence. Including his history, experience, skills, support system (like family and friends), mindset, emotional maturity, physical characteristics, etc. So, for example, if a man grew up gaining valuable experience under the oversight of supportive parents, he's likely to have more confidence than someone who doesn't have these advantages. This is the natural way we think of confidence developing.

But then there's another kind of confidence that doesn't depend on any of these factors–which is great news if they are missing from your life. We can call this a supernatural confidence that you are able to benefit from quickly, once you understand its spiritual source. The thought of experiencing this kind of confidence may seem inaccessible to ordinary men, but it's available to anyone who knows his true identity. Not only that, this type of confidence can become a dominant feature of your daily existence.

One of my favorite illustrations of this supernatural confidence is the Apostle Paul. A man with a strong pedigree, Paul's lineage goes back to the tribe of Benjamin. He was a Hebrew of Hebrews, and a Pharisee who was blameless with regard to the law (Phil. 3:4-6). This background gave Paul a solid basis for natural confidence, or what he called 'confidence in the flesh.' Yet after meeting Jesus, he no longer found his confidence here. In fact, he considered these things rubbish compared to knowing Him. Instead, his identity became firmly grounded in Christ, resulting in a distinct and potent form of confidence. Which empowered him to pursue world-changing goals, endure severe hardships, and confront ungodly leaders. It was this transformation of identity that shaped him into the Apostle Paul.

Don't miss the nature of the shift that took place in Paul's life after finding his new identity in Christ. He no longer based his confidence on credentials that attracted the world's attention, but on spiritual realities stemming from his relationship with God.

There's something else to notice about Paul's transformation that might challenge your conception of what it means to be a godly man. He didn't become a detached, ethereal figure who disengaged from the world. Instead, he became stronger in both his ability and zeal to engage it. This transformation was entirely due to where Paul found his identity, as he came to know who he truly was on a much deeper level.

Now here is something remarkable as it pertains to you and me. The Bible says we're to imitate Paul as he follows Christ (1 Cor. 11:1).

This would include imitating him in his confidence. But how do we do this? The answer is in the same way Paul did–by receiving and believing what God says about our identity. When Paul got his new identity, he didn't achieve it or earn it. It was bestowed on him as he saw and believed what was revealed to him. And the same is true of us. You don't get your God-given identity through the time you put in or effort you expend. You simply receive it by His grace. This is the secret to knowing who you really are, and experiencing all the blessings of God that go with it throughout your life.

The Gift of Your Identity
Your identity then is something you receive. And the possibility of receiving it is something the Bible speaks about clearly.

As we read in the gospel of John:

"But as many as received him, to them he gave the right to become children of God, even to those that believe in his name" (Jn. 1:12).

Notice what a strong identity statement this is. It says we have the right to become *children of God* by simply receiving Him as the true light which has come into the world. And the way we receive Him is by *believing*. Once we do, our identity is securely grounded in Him. And we can gain an appreciation of how secure we are in this position by remembering our adopted sonship in Christ is something God predestined before the foundation of the world (Eph. 1:4-5)!

The main point to take away from this is that your core identity–the essence of who you are–is a gift. This may be hard to conceive, as it's so common for people to get their identity from their accomplishments, roles or life story. But this truth is fundamental. It traces back to God's design for us to depend on Him, as creatures made in His image. And this truth is reaffirmed through the redemption that belongs to all who believe in Christ.

So then, our true identity is not something we construct, but something produced in us by God. We simply need to recognize and embrace this fact. And for this to occur, three things must take place.

Essentials for Receiving the Gift of Your Identity

First, you need to understand the truth that God made you in His image. There was a time when our culture widely acknowledged that God created us in His image and likeness, and this belief instilled a deep respect for human life. This consensus no longer exists, leading to a diminished awareness of this fundamental aspect of our nature. As a result, many people are left searching for their true identity. The good news is the truth about your creation and its significance for your identity is revealed and accessible. And recognizing this is the essential first step in receiving your identity as a gift.

Second, you need to see how this applies to you personally. People often assume that simply reading the right books, having the right ideas in mind, or agreeing with certain truth statements will change their life for the better. But you need something more. You must be convinced that the truth you are considering pertains to you and that you must respond to it. So as we continue our discussion about discovering your God-given identity, be sure to think about how everything we're considering applies to you. As you realize how all this affects you and how it answers your questions about your identity, you'll be in a position to move forward in a life-changing way. And this leads to the third step.

Third, you have to embrace and believe that what has been revealed is true and necessary for you. It isn't enough to hold certain facts in your mind or even deeply ponder these truths. You must reach the point where you stake your life on them, and live differently because of them. In short, you have to truly believe. This includes truths about your identity. Your consideration of your identity gets into the core of what you believe about yourself. Embracing these truths may require you to view yourself differently than you have before, or at least in a more nuanced manner, which might raise some questions. But as we look more fully at God's framework for your identity, and you consider this with a believing heart, I trust you'll see the pieces coming together to give you the full picture.

Before we get there though, I want to highlight a few ways receiving your identity as a gift from God will positively affect you.

Benefits of Receiving the Gift of Your Identity

No more chasing
A lot of people are on a chase to find their identity these days. The methods of their pursuit might include self-reflection, seeking feedback, counseling, therapy, travel, probing different spiritual beliefs or new areas of learning, and so on. Some take extreme measures, like casting off long-held convictions, exploring different sexualities, leaving a marriage or even trying to change one's gender. This quest to find one's identity is stressful and unsettling for those who are on it, because the objective can seem so elusive. Yet once someone discovers their identity is a gift from God and receives it, there's resolution. The chasing is over.

No more comparing
People often begin questioning their identity by comparing themselves to others. They look at the lives of others and become discontent and unsure about who they are. This starts them on a process of trying to solidify their identity, all while measuring themselves against those around them. The problem here is once you start comparing there's no end to it, because the standard you're looking at is always changing. So you never really arrive or land anywhere, and this means you're always vulnerable to the changing of the times and the pressures that go with it. But once you realize your identity is something fixed by God and you adopt it, the comparisons stop.

No more uncertainty
We live in a world where everything seems relative or subjective, with everyone having an opinion on what is right. This can fuel skepticism and uncertainty, casting doubt on nearly everything– including your own identity. But if we look at the world as created by God, accept the framework He has revealed in His Word, and see how what we observe and experience fits within that framework, then certainty becomes possible. And once you're certain about who you are, there's no more second-guessing where you belong or what you're meant to do. It sets you up to live your life and make the most of your gifts, just as God intends, right here in your own time and setting.

Peace and Contentment
Another benefit to add to these is the peace and contentment that's often missing these days. Trying to figure yourself out can be exasperating and exhausting. But, as you look to the Lord in faith and come to terms with your God-given identity, you come to a place of calmness and satisfaction. The wrestling with who you are

or who you're supposed to be is over. As your identity is settled, it brings rest.

Embracing your identity also puts you in a place of peace and contentment in your relationships with others. You recognize that the people in your life are not competitors or benchmarks for comparison, but partners to serve alongside in God's greater plan for humanity. This allows you to rejoice in the successes of others and support them in their struggles, all while remaining secure in your own identity.

And then, of course, there's also peace and contentment with God. When you quit seeking to construct your own identity and embrace the one God has for you, it brings oneness with Him. The striving ends, and in its place comes a life of trust in your Creator and Redeemer, as He fulfills His purpose through you.

Experiencing these benefits frees you to move forward and live out your part in God's story. Do you remember from the last chapter how I emphasized the importance of not letting your identity depend on certain elements of your story? That's still crucial to keep in mind. But, you *do* have a story that's unique and special, and it plays a significant role in the larger narrative God is unfolding in the world. And when you live your story from a secure identity, you will most effectively fulfill your place in His grand narrative, according to the purpose He has for you. This is true for anyone, no matter who you are.

Believing and Receiving is the Key
What I'm conveying about receiving your identity isn't complicated. The many voices in our culture makes it seem that finding your identity must be complex–only to be untangled through a lot of introspection or expert help. But discovering your identity

and building your life upon it really is straightforward. And it's my goal to help you see it this way.

One way to do this is by referring back to Abraham. I mentioned Abraham earlier as one who had an identity that equipped him to follow God wherever He led him. What I didn't mention is that this journey began with faith. "Abraham believed the Lord…" in all He told him and promised (Gen. 15:6). Then, because he believed, Abraham did whatever God directed him to do, which involved leaving his homeland and encountering many trails. Ultimately, Abraham–as an outcome of his faith-filled identity--did in fact became the 'father of many nations,' just as God said he would (Gen. 17:5).

This is one of the great stories of the Bible, and it's well-known to many. But the key takeaway here is that it all hinged on the simplicity of faith. Abraham's identity, his blessings, and the way he became a blessing to the world–all emerged from the simplicity of believing what God said.

I understand you may never have considered the connection between faith and your identity. It might seem that one belongs in the realm of religion and the other in psychology. However, this division is man-made, and it shouldn't hinder us from understanding how God created us as living souls. He's always intended for us to find our identity in Him and in the unique way He designed us. The key is believing Him. As we do, we discover that He already has the answers to the questions many are asking today about their identity.

To finish this section, I want to leave you with part of an interaction I had with a young friend of mine…

Dear Kyle,

I understand how all the talk about identity you're hearing in college is creating confusion and making you feel lost. You're not alone! As you seek to resolve this, I encourage you to go back to your roots. You've been given a good foundation during your years growing up in church and with your family. It may be covered up by the messages of our culture, but the training you received in your younger years have the answers you are looking for. That may be hard to see right now, but if you believe, you will. As St. Augustine pointed out long ago, belief leads us to understand.

Your friend,

David

This note reflects the struggle a lot of people, especially young adults, face today regarding their identity. Fortunately, Kyle resolved his identity crisis after revisiting teachings he had dismissed from his youth and engaging in some significant soul-searching. Now, he is growing in his faith and exploring how to best use his gifts in God's larger story.

Breakthrough Insight:
The only way to experience confidence in your identity is to receive it as a gift from God with a believing heart.

CHAPTER FIVE

WHY FINDING YOUR IDENTITY CAN SEEM SO HARD

I've expressed that discovering your God-given identity isn't complicated, and that you can certainly find it if you're looking in the right direction with a believing heart. I mention this because nowadays it seems everyone is seeking their identity somewhere other than where it truly lies.

They're looking for their identity somewhere in their story, in what they've achieved, or things that have happened to them. And, of course, there's a big push for people to find their identity in their gender or race, or even their feelings. Yet none of these are directions to go if you hope to possess the kind of thorough-going identity that positions you to fulfill God's purpose for your life.

Now you may wonder… If finding your identity is simple, why does it seem so elusive? And why are so many people looking for their identity in the wrong places? Good questions.

Knowing your true identity is straightforward and accessible to everyone willing to embrace it (we'll get into the details of this in the next section of the book). But, there is a catch! And the catch is this…

We Take Pride in Constructing Our Own Identity
As fallen individuals, we take satisfaction in defining our own identities, rather than accepting the gift of identity God has prepared for us. And we need grace to transform our hearts so that we can truly receive our true identity!

This may be hard to fathom, but we aren't naturally inclined to find our identity in what God has revealed to us. Instead, we are more disposed to derive our identity from something within our control. In other words, we prefer to establish our identity according to our own choosing and find it in something we've done, achieved, or experienced.

Consider a few common examples...

A man may have been athletic in his youth, and then continues to be physically active as an adult. He likes having a significant part of his identity come from being known as a middle-aged fit guy.

Or take a man who has devoted himself to building a thriving business, and now enjoys wealth and independence. He feels good about his accomplishment, and finds his identity in it.

And then there are those who see themselves as victims–either of a disease, some hardship, or an injustice–and they choose to build their identity upon their affliction.

All these examples share a common thread: these men have anchored their identity in various aspects of their personal stories. They find this approach gratifying, yet they're unaware it's blinding them to the identity that God, who created them, intends.

This type of thing also occurs when a man chooses to find his identity in one of the roles he fills. For example, a man might see himself as a sacrificial husband, having laid down his life for his wife in many ways. It's easy for him to wrap his identity in this role, as he points to all the things he has done and takes pride in being a 'good husband.'

What I'm aiming to get across is that we humans like our independence and control when it comes to our identity. We like to get credit for it too. This may seem like a natural course as we incorporate our personality, desires, creativity, gifts, opportunities and so on. But the truth is, when we base our identity on what we've done—or what may have happened to us—we miss the specially-crafted identity God has prepared for us.

This human preference goes back thousands of years, and we need to be aware of its influence on us today so we can see how it's a factor in our own hearts.

Why Refusing Your God-Given Identity Comes Easily
The first to abandon his God-given identity was Adam, back in the Garden of Eden. God created Adam with a specific identity and purpose. We'll dig deeper into this, but for now let's just note Adam rejected God's design. This not only severed his relationship with his Creator, it cut him off from the source of his identity.

Adam's choice seems illogical upon reflection. God created him as the pinnacle of His creation, to serve as His representative and co-regent over the earth (Psalm 8). There really couldn't have been a better and more honored place to exist within all that God had made! Yet, this wasn't sufficient for Adam. He didn't want to live within God's hierarchy; he desired more. When the temptation to be like God arose, he succumbed to it. And his rebellion has affected all of us ever since.

As Adam's offspring, we do the same thing he did. It comes easy to us. We too want to function independently from our Creator. And like Adam, we've become disconnected from the source of our identity and purpose. There's a part of us that likes it this way because we crave autonomy. Like the famous singer, we want to look back on our lives and say, "I did it my way." Yet deep down, we know doing it our way is what disorients us and leaves us wandering aimlessly.

Because of this condition, we are left to navigate our identity alone. So we tend to stumble through, trying to piece together an identity on our own or settling for whatever identity others assign to us. In our hearts, we're aware there is something more, leaving us feeling hollow and dissatisfied.

Of course, there is an alternative–that offers clarity, hope and confidence. And it comes to us as we trust God and believe what He's revealed about us. But pride is powerful. It's determined that we maintain independence from God, as we operate on our own terms. So pride in itself is enough to keep us from our God-given identity.

But there's another factor that makes finding our true identity difficult. Our culture exerts powerful forces that complicate the journey for men to embrace their God-given identity. Since these forces are so prevalent and influential, it's worth noting them. As we do, consider how they are affecting you.

Four Cultural Forces That Keep Men from Their God-Given Identity

First, men today are often viewed as inept and a problem. Consider, for example, how men are regularly portrayed as out of touch and incompetent on television programs and in movies. I can't count how many times I've seen a young man, husband or father depicted as clueless about how things work in today's world. This reinforces the idea that men should step aside, fostering a negative self-image and discouraging them from attempting to live in their true identity.

Another cultural force concerns the shifting dynamics in relationships between men and women. Traditionally, roles were clear-cut: men were seen as providers and protectors, while women focused on domestic responsibilities, such as childcare and household management. Nowadays, these roles have undergone a significant change.

Without getting into the pros and cons of these changes, one thing is clear: we've entered a world where it can appear women don't need men anymore. After all, it's not unusual these days for a woman to earn more than her husband. Women also have concealed carry permits and good home security systems to keep themselves safe. Developments like these offer advantages for many women, but it's left many men questioning their identity and purpose.

A third area where culture influences men's identity is our tendency to question or resist certainty. Today, if a man expresses convictions about anything, including his own identity, he often faces pushback. In the current climate of negative portrayals of men, confidence can be perceived as stubbornness or closed-mindedness. Regrettably, this is often how assertive men are met. And as men recognize these dynamics, they may struggle with how to perceive themselves and withdraw, resulting in a lack of defined character and diminished strength.

Finally, one other cultural influence to note is the lack of substantial biblical teaching on masculinity. This absence is especially conspicuous in churches, which are in the best position to give instruction about God's design for men (and women). This, no doubt, has occurred alongside our culture's shift toward more egalitarian thinking. The point to take away from this is that the lack of instruction on identity issues has been detrimental, leaving men ill-equipped to respond to the cultural pressures on their identities.

Collectively, these forces disconnect men from their God-given identity and influence them to simply go along with the downward drift of the culture, which only compounds their struggle to live with a clear sense of biblical, masculine identity.

Today's Identity Advocates
There are some who have responded to our culture's confusion about identity by approaching the issue with missionary zeal. These 'identity advocates' make it their mission to encourage others to question assumptions about their identity and explore alternatives. These advocates commonly appear on social media, in popular culture, corporate boardrooms, and in the classroom as well. Their message may have a strong appeal due to its seeming respect for human individuality, but it never leads people to the eternal truth about their identity.

In a culture that increasingly rejects God and His order, this can lead to some extreme positions and unfortunate outcomes for those seeking to validate their identity. A striking example is the matter of attempting to change one's gender. Like many, you might find this phenomenon hard to understand. But it exemplifies the pattern of determining one's identity independently from our Creator, much like Adam did.

So, there are a number of ways someone can get off-course when it comes to their identity. On one end of the spectrum, you might passively accept the cultural norms coming against you. On the other end, you might pursue whatever identity appeals to you. In any case, *if you are choosing your identity on your own–rather than receiving the one God has for you–you're going to end up off-track.*

Your identity is like a compass. If you have your bearings straight from the beginning, you're going to head in the right direction. But if they're off from the start, you'll be misdirected the whole way and end up far from the destination God has in mind for you.

This is why Jesus emphasized the importance of building on the right foundation in His Sermon on the Mount (Mt. 7:24-29). Here He compares acting on His teaching to building a house on rock, while ignoring His words like building on sand. Similarly, anchoring your identity in what God has revealed in the Bible results in a solid sense of self, whereas neglecting this leads to an unstable one.

So whether you think in terms of a compass or a foundation, your identity is a crucial starting point for your entire life.

Because the identity we build our lives upon has major consequences, and we often seek to base it on our preferences, we must further examine why we have difficulty landing on our true identity. This issue points back to our tendency toward pride.

Pride and the Need for Grace
Pride lies at the heart of the struggle we face with our identity. It's a constant presence, lurking beneath the surface, urging us to live life on our own terms. This is a universal challenge stemming from our fallen nature, and something we all must confront. Overcoming it requires seeking God's help, acknowledging our pride, and humbling ourselves before Him. Only then can we embrace what He has revealed about ourselves and find hope in His guidance.

For this to happen, we need His grace to open our eyes, so we can see what we're really like and observe our resistance to live according to His design. And once our eyes are open, we need more grace to humbly receive the identity He has for us.

We must confront a harsh reality: we are enslaved to following our own path, even when we recognize the truth and understand its consequences. Such is the power of our pride. But, when we humble ourselves and receive our place in God's created order, He sets us free to live in the power of our true identity, which is essential for living the life He intends for us.

So to make the point of this chapter clear…

Finding your identity need not be difficult. God isn't hiding it from you. But we all have a proud, fallen nature that complicates the process. It's the catch we all have to face, as this nature inclines us to find our identity on our own terms. Yet with God's help, we can overcome this obstacle, embrace our true identity, and fulfill the purpose He has had for us all along.

In explaining this challenge to finding your identity, I'm reminded of the legend of Faust, the discontented scholar who strikes a deal with the devil in exchange for unlimited knowledge and worldly pleasures. Initially gratified, Faust soon realizes that his pride and willingness to compromise have left him empty. This tale resembles the man who tries to find his identity in his achievements or experiences, rather than God. While initially satisfying, these 'glory days' leave him wanting.

Since we are considering obstacles to finding your identity, there is one more crucial point I'd like to make.

A Caveat

When I talk about discovering your identity, it might seem like I'm suggesting you need to uncover some hidden or esoteric knowledge about yourself that will bring enlightenment or salvation. This idea resembles the ancient heresy of gnosticism, which teaches salvation through knowledge. But my stance differs. We need more than just information, knowledge, or special insight. We need transformation.

I trust this chapter has made this evident.

It's not enlightenment we need, it's regeneration—a new heart, a new birth, and a new way of seeing. This is the way to a transformed identity. And it echoes the main point of the last chapter: that our identity is a gift, available to all who humbly receive it.

In the next section, we're going to look at the foundation of your identity in detail. But before jumping into that, I encourage you to consider:

Do you genuinely desire the identity that God has prepared for you? Are you ready to humble yourself to receive it?

Breakthrough Insight:

Your God-given identity is ready and waiting for you. Don't let pride get in the way of receiving it.

PART TWO

Your Identity's Foundation

CHAPTER SIX

THE BASIS OF YOUR IDENTITY

The nature of our identity is something we tend to complicate. We rely on subjective feelings that never bring certainty, rather than focusing on the essence of what makes us who we are. We can resolve this by realizing our identity is an objective reality God has built into us from the beginning. Our waywardness has taken us away from this truth, leading us to uncertainty about our true selves. But thankfully, God, in his determination to restore us, graciously gives us eyes to see and hearts to believe, so we can know who we are and function accordingly.

Seeing the reality of what God has created, how we have fallen, and the redemption He provides is the core mechanism that leads us to our true identity. And discerning how this applies personally is crucial for any man to experience the self-understanding and engagement with the world God intends for him.

To illustrate the working of this mechanism and set the stage for its explanation, imagine the following scenario…

As a father, you give a valuable gift to your son. You know he may not appreciate the value of the gift, but you give it to him anyway. With the gift, you supply instructions on how to use it and get the most benefit from it. Then, to your disappointment, you find your son misusing the gift. In fact, he uses the gift in a way that's completely contrary to its intent, and it breaks. As the one who gave him the gift, you're grieved. Yet despite this setback, you do not give up on your son regarding the gift. You know that possessing it is essential for his well-being, so you do whatever it takes to restore it to him. Not only that, you have a plan for your son to gain a new appreciation for the gift, so he can use it to bring about the good you always envisioned.

This mirrors the situation we encounter with our God-given identity. From the beginning, God has given mankind the unique identity that comes from being His special creation. But since the days of Adam, we've misused this gift. Yet God has determined there will be those who receive His grace and live according to the design He has for them, so they can participate in His plan to bring blessing to the world.

Let's unpack this further so you can see how this mechanism works and serves as the foundation of your identity. As we move forward, you might find it helpful to keep in mind the words *created, fractured,* and *restored* as a way to think about the progression of your identity. We'll begin by looking at the first foundational aspect, which has to do with the creation or origin of your identity.

I. Your Identity Created

In the beginning, God set the mold for mankind with a specific design. The Bible describes this as being 'fearfully and wonderfully made' (Psalm 139:14), which is an apt description. There is something absolutely unique and remarkable about human beings, and Scripture attributes this to being made in God's image, or the *imago Dei.*

The Bible tells of the formation of this image in Genesis 1:26, where God says *"Let Us make mankind in Our image, according to Our likeness..."*

Here you have the Father, the Son, and the Holy Spirit consulting together about how to create mankind. They deliberate about what kind of creature to make and they decide to create humans, a little lower than God, in their own image and likeness. They did this for a specific purpose, which we'll get into later. For now, notice and remember: God made us in His image.

So what does it mean to be made in His image?

Theologians have considered this for centuries. At its most basic level, bearing God's image has to do with reflecting His nature and character. Taking a closer look, it involves having certain godlike characteristics or attributes as a part of our makeup. Here are the main ones.

Awareness of eternity
The Bible tells us God has put eternity in our hearts (Ecc. 3:11). So we have in our being an awareness of the future and a sense of eternity like no other member of creation. You can notice this in yourself in the way you ponder and plan for the future. You can also see it whenever you perceive the weightiness and long-term consequences of your decisions.

Desire for justice
Every human being has an innate sense of fairness or what is right, which we call justice. While our opinions on what is just may differ, it is a universally held ideal because God has made it part of His image in us. The Bible explains this by saying He has written the basic standards of His law on our hearts (Rom. 2:15).

Sense of morality
We inherently recognize that certain things are good and others are evil. For example, there's little debate that sacrificial love is good

and murder is bad. This sense of morality is evident in how your conscience may accuse or defend you regarding certain actions. While sin distorts our moral faculties, our moral nature is never erased.

Ability to reason
The ability to think logically also goes along with being made in God's image. The Lord Himself engages us in this capacity when He says, "Come now, let us reason together" (Isa. 1:14). The ability to reason is a complex cognitive process that involves analyzing, evaluating, making decisions and solving problems. It's something we often take for granted, but it's a fundamental aspect of being an image-bearer of God.

Capacity to love
God made us to love, or to have affections and make commitments toward people, ideals and Himself. This love is a significant motivating factor, which leads us to work, obey, sacrifice and even lay down our lives for that which we believe in and care about. All humanity values love. It's a universal language. Which isn't surprising, since we're all made in the image of the one who is love (1 Jn. 4:8).

Creative impulse
This last feature isn't always highlighted in discussions about the image of God, but I believe it's crucial. God made us with a drive to create, build, and develop the world around us. This impulse is evident in children as soon as they have the motor skills to express themselves. Our lives are most satisfying when we harness this inclination to its fullest extent, regardless of our age.

All these qualities are foundational to your true identity. It's not hard to see them at work in your own life, as well as in the lives of those around you. An awareness of eternity, a desire for justice, a sense of morality, the ability to reason, to love, and to create–these are all evident and play a major part in defining who we are.

By the way, these remarkable human attributes serve as evidence for the existence of God, as they demonstrate the work of a wise and powerful designer. I am convinced it requires greater faith to believe these characteristics arose by random chance than by the hand of a sovereign Creator.

Back to our topic at hand, our unique design as those made in God's image reveals He has supplied a one of a kind foundation for our identity. One that's suited for not only relating to Him, but carrying out His purpose in the world.

Unfortunately, mankind hasn't done a great job using the gift of our identity for the purpose God gave it. Because of the Fall, this is true for all of us, leading to the second foundational aspect of our identity to consider.

> **Pause to Apply:** What aspects of God's image reflected in you helps you see your unique design as a person?

II. Your Identity Fractured

When God made mankind, He set us up for success. But, Adam, vulnerable to temptation, rejected his place in God's order and strayed from His plan for him. This fall separated Adam from his Creator, fractured his identity, and brought death into the world. In the process, Adam lost the fundamental understanding of who he was and his purpose.

From that time forward, every man inherits the same situation. We are born separated from God, broken in our identity, and unaware of who God truly made us to be. This has left us on our own to put the pieces of our lives together, as we seek to figure out who we are and what our lives are about. In this condition, we resort to various coping mechanisms and self-expressions that hinder us from living the life God intends for us. It's important to acknowledge these struggles as they affect us all in our daily lives..

Guilt and shame
Adam and his wife are known for trying to hide from God and cover up their shame after they sinned. As sons and daughters of Adam, we seek to do the same when we know we've done wrong and are guilty. We hide. We isolate. We go it alone. And carrying this burden of guilt and shame is a fact of life for all who are living with a broken identity.

Blame Shifting
Something that stands out about Adam is that he wouldn't take responsibility for his actions. Instead, he blamed Eve, and even suggested God was at fault. We've all been afflicted with this tendency to deny responsibility, just like Adam. We see it everywhere–in relationships, business, and politics, for example–all the time. And our inclination to blameshift pushes us further away from our God-given identity, because He created us to be responsible beings before Him.

Fear and cowardice
Fear and cowardice arise when we're uncertain about our identity, leading to a failure to act and protect. Again, Adam set the pattern. In Genesis 2:15, God instructed Adam to safeguard the garden. But as he doubted the identity God gave him, he lacked the courage and resolve to confront the serpent when necessary. Instead of protecting

Eve by defeating the snake as he should have, he succumbed to its deception and lies.

Anger and aggression
The fall of mankind affects not just how we think about our own identity, but how we view others. And this can lead us to act out with anger or ungodly aggression toward those in our midst. This happened soon after Adam's fall, when Cain–out of a lack of faith–murdered his brother Abel (Gen. 4). And this same principle of disregarding the image of God in others is often at work in our own anger.

Making a name for yourself
God created us to find our identity in Him. Apart from Him, we often seek to establish our identity by making a name for ourselves, surpassing others, and proving our superiority. This spirit goes all the way back to the Tower of Babel, where its builders sought to make a name for themselves in competition with God (Gen. 11). Ultimately, God judged this effort by bringing confusion among the people. And it makes one wonder how much confusion regarding our identities today can be traced to our attempts to find them outside of Him.

When you consider these effects of our fractured identity, you can see how our understanding and functioning according to the way God made us has been marred. Recognizing this is an important–albeit negative–part of discovering your own God-given identity because it makes plain the need for His help. This brings us to the third foundational aspect of our identity to consider, which offers the hope of restoration.

> **Pause to Apply:** What are some of the ways the fracturing of your identity is evident to you?

III. Your Identity Restored

One of the biggest indicators of the breadth of God's mercy is that He has not left us alone in our broken condition. He certainly could have, and who would blame Him? But He chose instead to restore us to Himself and make us whole again. So right after Adam's fall, He initiated a plan to recover what was ruined and lost. And the success of this plan was ensured through a second Adam, Jesus Christ, by way of His life, death and resurrection.

Part of this plan involved restoring our God-given identity.

When we reflect on what Jesus has done for us, we immediately think in terms of the forgiveness and salvation He brings. And He indeed brings these things. Jesus confirms this in saying, "Truly, truly I say to you, he who hears my word, and believes him who sent me has eternal life and does not come into judgment is passed out of death into life" (John 5:24).

But Jesus came to do more than bring forgiveness and eternal life. He came to restore everything wrecked by the Fall. He came to renew all things (Rev. 21:5), and this includes our identity.

One way to think about this is in terms of sonship. The power of sonship is something every man can identify with, since we all have earthly fathers. And your own particular experience with your father can greatly affect whether you live as an orphan or experience the benefits of a true son.

An orphan lacks a sense of belonging and often faces unstable circumstances, so he's constantly striving for approval to survive. In contrast, a true son is firmly grounded and secure in his position, and this enables him to live with confidence, experience rest, and enjoy the fullness of his gifts, as he's assured of his acceptance.

Just recognizing this difference can totally reorient a man's life. It can also determine whether he flourishes or languishes. And here's the really good news. As mentioned earlier, through faith in Christ, you are made a son of God as He adopts you into His family.

And not only that, the Holy Spirit confirms that this is so, as the promise of Scripture tells us:

The Spirit Himself bears witness with our spirit that we are children of God (Rom. 8:16).

With these words, all who believe are assured of a new identity, along with all the benefits that come with it—regardless of their past. Through faith, you are not only a son and heir who belongs to God, but also His workmanship, created to do good works (Eph. 2:10). And as God's original design is restored, you are in position to fulfill His purpose in the specific place He has for you.

Pause to Apply: In what ways can you envision living with a restored identity making a difference in your life?

From the Designer's Perspective
A good way to see the significance of your God-given identity is to think of it from the perspective of its Designer.

In our society, we are familiar with various products, each meticulously planned by a designer before being manufactured. During this planning process, each product is given detailed specifications to carry out its purpose. Only after these specifications are carefully considered does production begin. Once completed, a product is identifiable by its function, allowing us to distinguish between hammers, toasters, and cars. And we understand that using a toaster to drive a nail would both damage the toaster and fail to drive the nail.

In a similar way, God has carefully planned the making of mankind. Even down to males and females, who share His image while having meaningful differences. And because of their differences are able to be fruitful, multiply, fill the earth and subdue it together under His oversight.

Failing to acknowledge God as the supreme Designer and living outside of His blueprint not only dishonors Him but also harms us, as it prevents us from fulfilling the purpose for which we've been created. On the other hand, embracing our God-given identity as those made in His image and remade through Jesus Christ is the core mechanism by which we discover who we are and fulfill God's purpose for our lives. Everything about knowing who we are and what God wants us to do starts with this.

In the next chapter, we'll take this a step further and explore the larger purpose for which God made us in His image and gave us our identity. It's within this framework that we each find our place in the world, with a self-image that honors Him and brings meaning to all we do.

Breakthrough Insight:
The foundation of your identity lies in the fact you've been created as an image-bearer of God. Our fall into sin has marred this image and distorted our sense of who we are. But a restored image and identity is available to all who receive the gift of redemption through faith in Jesus Christ.

CHAPTER SEVEN

A BIBLICAL FRAMEWORK FOR LIVING

Unfortunately, few men have a very developed framework for understanding their existence in today's world. This chapter aims to provide one, based on what God has revealed in His Word.

Having a biblical framework for life–that's rooted in an understanding of His creation–is crucial. Without it, men's lives become focused solely on fulfilling obligations and desires.The obligations encompass responsibilities like going to work, paying the bills, taking care of the family, and so on. The desires cover things like food, relaxation, sports, sex, hobbies and whatever particular interests a man may have.

Facing this, a man who practices even a little self-reflection eventually begins to wonder about the meaning of his life. It's like Solomon who, after completing a variety of building projects, described it as vanity or chasing after the wind (Ecc. 2:11). This state of futility leaves men disheartened, demoralized and disconnected. Disheartened because they no longer see the point to what they're doing. Demoralized because they can't envision anything changing for the better. And disconnected because men without a clear sense of purpose usually end up retreating and isolating themselves.

But not all is gloomy. As a man finds himself in this situation, his eyes open to the need for a more profound worldview for his life. This puts him in a place to see the framework provided by His

Creator. And as he receives this with a believing heart, he has the capacity to carry on a completely transformed life.

There are three different facets of this framework a man must embrace for this transformation to occur in his life. The first of these is God-given revelation.

Facet One: God-Given Revelation
The only way for us to know anything about God and His intent for us is through what He reveals. Thankfully, He reveals Himself in a couple of ways.

First, God reveals Himself through His creation or nature. The Bible describes this self-disclosure by stating, "The heavens declare the glory of God" (Psalm 19:1). This revelation plainly shows God's existence and is so powerful it leaves everyone without excuse. From the beginning of creation, His invisible qualities, eternal power and divine nature, have been clearly seen, being understood from what He has made (Rom. 1:20).

From God's creation, we can see that this is His world and we are a part of it. But natural revelation alone doesn't tell us what life in this world is all about. To understand our place and purpose, we need something more. And God has provided this in His second form of revelation: the Bible. In it, He lays out the grand narrative of what He has done and the big picture of what He is doing. The Bible also reveals His design and directs us how we are to live.

God's revelation in the Bible gives us essential truths about the nature of God, ourselves, why we are here, and what we're supposed to do. By filling in the details natural revelation leaves out, it shows us the way.

In sum, Scripture is the guide we need, and it testifies to this when it says...

All Scripture is inspired by God and profitable for teaching, for reproof, for correction, and for training in righteousness (2 Tim. 3:16).

This special form of revelation doesn't diminish the importance of creation. By studying creation, we discover the intricacies of what God has made and how the world works. The knowledge we've accumulated over centuries has not only enriched our lives but also played a vital part in fulfilling the purpose God has for us (more on that soon). But, it's only the special revelation of His Word that gives us what we need to answer the fundamental questions of life. It alone reveals the divine framework for understanding who we are and why we exist. Apart from this biblical framework, we see things in bits and pieces and fail to grasp God's big picture for life in His world.

At this point I should pause, because you may be a reader who wonders, "Why should I believe God's revelation?"

Most convincing to me is that the Bible is self-attesting. It makes its truthfulness apparent as the Spirit bears witness to our spirits, showing that the Bible is consistent with what we observe in the world. From the grandeur of creation to the depravity of man to the power of love, everything confirms Scripture's explanation of reality. In other words, God's revelation is in sync with life as we know it. And the Spirit testifies to this truth in our hearts.

Receiving this revelation as truth is the starting point for living within the framework God has established. Within it, we discover who we are and why we're here. This brings us to facet number two of His framework.

> **Pause to Apply:** Do you embrace the Bible as God's authoritative guide for your life?

Facet Two: God-Given Identity
In the Bible, God reveals a number of creational norms. These are givens that tell us how God made and ordered the world. They are what we might consider 'fixed realities' and address issues like the nature of men and women, the place of work and rest, the goodness and fruitfulness of creation, and so on. Among the most basic creational norms is that of man's identity.

God made us in a certain, distinct way. As Creator, this is His prerogative. Scripture illustrates this with the metaphor of the potter and the clay (Jer. 18). As the potter, God is free to form us, the clay, into whatever He desires, and for whatever purpose He sees fit. It was His deliberate choice to make us in His image and likeness, equipping us to live in communion with Him, represent Him, and fulfill His purpose in the world. This truth underlies our identity as human beings. And embracing it enables us to live fully, as we acknowledge our dependence on our Creator and operate within His design.

I want to emphasize that there's a goodness to God's design that is often overlooked. So all the creational norms God established–like marriage between a man and a woman, the bringing forth of children, working to develop the earth, living out our identity as His image-bearers, and taking time to rest–are part of His plan to bring blessing to the world. There is nothing oppressive about it. We just need to receive these norms with believing hearts.

But the problem from Adam onwards is that we've failed to believe and receive. We've adopted an "I know better than God" disposition, which has led to what one theologian calls a 'flight from humanity.' In this state, we seek to escape God's creational norms, and define our identity and reason for existing on our own terms. The effect of this has been dehumanizing for all of us, as we've lost our appreciation of what it means to be human beings–uniquely made in His image, with an identity and purpose found in Him.

Surely you can see the effects of this yourself. Not only in the individual suffering you observe around you, but also in the way society has become less considerate of people. As we've disconnected from God as the source of our identity, we've devalued what it means to be human.

We also now have a push toward transhumanism, with its attempts to transcend our natural, God-intended limitations by technological means. And, there are also political expressions of this problem, with an elite ruling class seeking to control the masses without regard to their humanity.

This scenario definitely makes finding and maintaining your true identity a challenge. Especially since what I just described has been institutionalized–in schools, government, media, popular culture and more. So if you are struggling with your own identity, it is not surprising. There's a lot coming against you, and you are not alone.

But don't despair, or depart from your journey to uncover your true identity and purpose. Through His Son, God provided the way for us to realign our humanity with the divine blueprint He established at the beginning of creation. And this restoration of our human nature is a crucial aspect of the gospel message. Since the link between the gospel and our identity may seem unfamiliar, let's explore it further.

When we hear the word 'gospel' we typically think in terms of grace, forgiveness, redemption, eternal life, etc. This makes sense, since these are all essential to what Jesus has come to bring us. But this is not all. He also came to restore our true identity, reestablish our personhood, and recover our position under God as we live life in His world.

We can understand this more clearly by elaborating a bit on the difference between the first and second Adam. God created the first Adam in His image to rule and cultivate the earth with Him. But Adam refused the place God had given him, fracturing his identity and leaving him to live as an orphan rather than a son. Yet, with the second Adam, who is Jesus, something different occurred. Here, God took on human flesh to become a greater Adam, who would recover what was lost by the first Adam. Jesus accomplished this completely, bringing not only forgiveness and eternal life but also a restored relationship and renewed mission with the Father for all who believe.

This restoration is the cornerstone of living in your true identity within God's framework for us today. And embracing it by faith is all you need to experience life as a new creation, with a remade identity in Christ (2 Corinthians 5:17).

Yet to live fully within the framework God has designed for you, there is one more facet to consider and embrace.

> **Pause to Apply:** How do you see the gospel as good news when it comes to your own identity?

Facet Three: God-Given Purpose

Your God-given identity is at the core of who you are, but this identity is not an end in itself. God created us with the identity and design He has for a reason–it serves as the means to fulfilling a larger purpose.

This is easy for us to comprehend as his image-bearers. We too craft things with particular designs for specific reasons. We make refrigerators to preserve food, stoves to cook meals, and plastic containers to store leftovers. How did we get the ability to do such things, and with such purpose? It comes from being made in the likeness of our Creator.

So, for what purpose did God make us? The Bible tells us early on in its first chapter, when it says we're to get dominion over all creation as co-rulers with Him.

Then God blessed them, and God said to them, "Be fruitful and multiply; fill the earth and subdue it; have dominion over the fish of the sea, over the birds of the air, and over every living thing that moves on the earth" (Gen. 1:28).

This verse presents what's known as the dominion or cultural mandate. We can add this mandate to the number of creational norms I mentioned earlier, as it's 'by design' that humanity would develop the world in cooperation with its Creator.

The Bible expands on the nature of this commission when it reveals how God told Adam to 'cultivate and keep' the Garden of Eden (Gen. 2:15). This means that Adam was given the task of developing and protecting the garden. This garden, of course, was just a starting point. As humanity has multiplied, we have inherited the same purpose to gardenize the whole earth with God. And this explains all the development we've seen take place through history, right up to today.

This is the purpose for which God designed humanity, shedding light on why He created us as He did: to be adequately equipped to carry out the tasks He has assigned to us, working in collaboration with Him.

I hope this resonates with you, especially If you could use some direction and encouragement. Men need and seek a clear purpose to express their capacity to create and protect. They also have a natural desire to achieve and accomplish meaningful goals, reflecting the image in which we've been made and the identity we've been given. The Fall damaged our ability to perceive our identity and twisted our purpose, leading to confusion and the misuse of our gifts. Yet Jesus–through the work of the Spirit–restores us and our abilities, not only promising eternal life but also enabling us to fulfill our purpose within God's mandate to extend His dominion in the world. This overall framework explains the reality of the world as it is and shows how a man can find his place and make his life count within it. This is something many thoughtful men I know are seeking, as they want to grasp the big picture and understand where they fit in. The biblical framework I've presented in this chapter offers just that.

A Biblical Framework for Living

> **Pause to Apply:** How does God's intent for us to get dominion with Him give direction and meaning to what you do?

Two Big Questions

Here's a summary of what I'm saying. There are two big questions every man wants answered (and I'm assuming this includes you!). The first question is "Who am I?" The second is "What am I supposed to do?" Not every man will verbalize these questions, but all will wonder about them in their hearts. If they don't have the answers, it will inhibit them from becoming who God intends them to be. It's also likely to discourage and frustrate them, leading many men to disengage and check out.

But God has provided the answer to both of these questions. Plainly. And I've presented the answers here. So if you are wondering who you are, you can know you are a unique creation of God, made in his image, which is where your identity is grounded. And, if you are wondering what you're supposed to do with your life, you can know God has put you here to fulfill your role in His dominion mandate, in your place and time.

Once a man is able to answer these two questions for himself, he's ready to live the life God has prepared for him. He has a solid reason to get up in the morning, since he knows who he is and what he's supposed to do. And this is extremely fulfilling too, because it allows a man to see how the effort He puts forth in employing his gifts has meaning and can make a difference.

At a time when many men are sitting on the sidelines, questioning their identity and purpose, this is very good news. It shows that God has revealed what we need. And once embraced, this empowers men to engage their world in ways they likely never have been before. It moves them from a life of introspection to actively using their gifts to impact the world around them.

Self-Image

As you think about applying this framework in your own life, it will help to say a little about the subject of self-image.

Self-image is a topic we hear a lot about. Discussions on the topic sometimes make Christians uneasy because they assume it reflects self-absorption or narcissism, which faithful believers want to avoid. However, considering one's self-image isn't the same as being consumed with oneself. It simply involves how you perceive yourself as a unique individual. That's what I want to address here, and offer a specific perspective on how to view yourself.

There are many factors that affect one's self-image. These include appearance, personality, social status, abilities and achievements, experiences, relationships, beliefs, values, attitudes, comparisons you make, and how you interpret or evaluate your thoughts. It's widely recognized that all of these factors can have a big influence on whether someone has what we'd call a positive or negative self-image.

But here, I'd like to offer a different approach. And I encourage you to see your self-image not as arising from these common factors, but from the framework we've examined in this chapter. This perspective has three major implications for your own self-image.

1) You see yourself as created in God's image and likeness, designed to exercise dominion in the world as you live in communion with Him.

2) You recognize that you have rebelled against God's design, resulting in various problems, but you have been redeemed and made a new man in Christ.

3) You understand that because of God's grace, you are now empowered to use your gifts and opportunities to contribute to building His kingdom in this present time.

When a man bases his self-image on these realities, all other factors of how he may see himself become less significant. They simply don't matter much. This makes him stronger and more stable in understanding who he is (identity), and positions him to enter into what God has given him to do (purpose). It also makes him less reactive to the opinions of others and better equipped to handle life's challenges.

But you've got to embrace this for yourself. As I said at the beginning of this chapter, many men lack the framework they need to make sense of their place in the world today. You don't have to be one of them. God has revealed what you need. It's yours to believe and receive.

Breakthrough Insight:
With God's revelation as the basis, you can adopt a framework for living that encompasses both your identity and purpose, knowing it's been crafted by your Creator.

CHAPTER EIGHT

ESSENTIAL ELEMENTS OF A STRONG IDENTITY

So far we've covered the idea that your identity–or how you view yourself–is at the core of living out God's plan for you. A big part of this is seeing yourself as He sees you and understanding how He designed you to live. This makes your identity a hook upon which an awful lot hangs, so it's in your interest to make sure it's as strong as can be.

In this chapter I'm going to give you the essential elements necessary for forming a strong identity.

To begin, take heart: anyone can possess a strong sense of identity–regardless of their background, status, or current circumstances.

Yet, no one acquires a strong identity overnight. There are ways of thinking, feeling and approaching situations that need transforming. So just as it takes some time to get your body in shape, reconditioning your identity requires patience and self-awareness. So be prepared to invest time and effort in the Spirit's process of renewing you from the inside out.

Beware of these longtime foes
As we get going, I should remind you of something I mentioned earlier. There's a lot coming against you that can make adopting your God-given identity challenging. To expand on this, there are three

longtime, seasoned foes who are intent on quashing your efforts toward arriving at your true identity and becoming a new man. These are the old-time enemies known as the world, the flesh, and the devil.

This world, as a system, functions in hostility to God and His plan for humanity. And those with earthly power work overtime to manipulate and deceive you into conforming. This is hard to resist, as most of us crave acceptance and recognition. We like to fit in. But if we're enslaved by worldly approval, we become trapped and miss living in our true identity and the important purpose God has for us. Be on guard against conforming to the world, and instead be transformed by the constant renewing of your mind (Rom. 12:2).

Your own flesh also works contrary to you. This principle of resistance lies within us all and constantly seeks to have us act independently from God. Driven by pride, the flesh wants to gratify every impulse, desire and promise of pleasure. Yet its ultimate aim is our ruin. Even if the flesh falls short of this goal, it can produce a lot of rotten fruit in our lives. So it's crucial to stay in step with the Spirit to live in our true identity and bear His life-giving fruit (Gal. 5:16-18).

The last enemy coming against you is the devil. This adversary is pre-eminent among our foes, going back to the Garden in his attempt to overthrow God's design for us. From the beginning, he's been a liar and deceiver. Today, deception and lies remain his primary methods to obscure our true identity and hinder us from living in its power. And by these means, he seeks to fulfill his mission is to steal, kill, and destroy. So, resist the devil and submit to God and His truth as you find your identity in Him (Jas. 4:7).

Essential Elements of a Strong Identity

> **Pause to Apply:** Which of these foes – world, flesh, or devil – do you anticipate giving you the most trouble as you seek to grow stronger in your identity?

These adversaries are relentless in their efforts to undermine God's plan for the human race, including His plan for you. So knowing how to handle them is essential, and a basic aspect of preparation is growing stronger in your identity. In this chapter we'll look at three critical components to help you become established in your own God-given identity.

These elements are worth revisiting often. Doing so will help you live in alignment with your Creator's intent for you. Like points on a compass or markers on the shore, they will guide you on the journey of fulfilling the purpose God has for your life. Put another way, finding and living in your identity is not a one-time event. It's something you're always maintaining and growing into as you deepen in understanding and faith. This requires vigilance, but it's not wearisome because you'll be making new discoveries about God's design, goodness and care for you. And you'll also see yourself becoming a more effective instrument in His kingdom.

ESSENTIAL ELEMENT #1: YOUR CORE CONVICTIONS

What you believe is at the foundation of having a strong identity. So take care to maintain your core convictions. Here I'm referring specifically to truths we've already covered in this book. I mention them again here because they are so important to living with a strong identity, and I encourage you to hide them in your heart.

To review, these core convictions are:

You've Been Created in God's Image
God has made you with a unique design, specially devised to relate to Him and carry out your purpose in the world. Your identity starts here.

You've Been Made for Dominion
God has created you to fulfill your part in advancing His kingdom, as you use your gifts and opportunities where He has you. This is the basis of your purpose.

You've Been Redeemed by Christ
God has not left you, even though you've tried to function without Him. He reclaims all who believe through His Son and restores them to their true identity and purpose.

Notice how together these core convictions set the context for your life as they ground you in the past, give meaning to the present, and vision for the future. Hopefully, they inspire you as well, as you see God is not finished with you. In fact, He may be just getting started to use you to the fullest!

Ideally, these core convictions are instilled during the earliest years of a child's life through family and a faithful church community. The Bible instructs those who possess God's words to not only treasure them in their hearts but also to teach them diligently to their children (Dt. 6:6-7). This is clearly intended to pass on the faith and provide children with needed spiritual instruction. Yet it also serves to establish the identity of the next generation–beginning at a young age–as they come to identify with being a part of the people of God.

But, in today's world, passing beliefs from one generation to the next usually falls short of this ideal. Most children receive minimal biblical instruction, particularly concerning their identity. And, what is passed on to children can have a negative impact, leaving them burdened with emotional baggage and uncertainty about who they are as they enter adulthood.

So where does this leave most people today? Many individuals who haven't had their identity positively instilled, or who are feeling the negative effects of their upbringing, experiences, or circumstances, are likely unsure of their identity. Some may even admit to feeling lost, which explains much of the confusion and uncertainty about identity today.

But here's the thing: anyone, at any age, can have their identity shaken, especially when facing a major life change or crisis. Over the years, I've spoken with many people who, after events like a business failure, divorce, or the loss of a loved one, had to reassess who they were. The good news is that times of crisis often lead to the development of a stronger identity. This process begins by revisiting and reinforcing core beliefs, which highlights the importance of regularly returning to these convictions to maintain a strong sense of identity.

You can begin applying this yourself by considering a few questions: How have my core beliefs developed? How have they changed? Where do they need to be reinforced? Take time with these questions, as the strength of your identity ultimately rests on your core beliefs.

ESSENTIAL ELEMENT #2: LIVING IN KEEPING WITH YOUR CORE CONVICTIONS

It's one thing to ascribe to certain core beliefs, but building a strong identity requires living consistently with them. Our convictions are not meant to be something we just write in a journal or store on a computer file and then forget. To truly benefit from them, we must commit to certain standards and habits. There's a direct correlation here: as your character grows, so will the strength of your identity. Conversely, if you become lax and start living outside of your core convictions, your sense of identity will weaken. In short, living a godly life makes for a strong identity.

Self-sabotage
A common problem among many men is self-sabotage. These men mentally acknowledge certain beliefs, but then make choices that contradict those beliefs. This behavior undermines their identity and ability to function effectively as men, resulting in outcomes that are both sad and frustrating. Let's look at a couple examples to see how this works.

James has a well-paying but dead-end job. He's developed valuable skills and has long thought about starting his own business. Changes in the economy and his company have convinced him the time is right, and after a lot of prayer and planning, he's ready to make the move. He's excited too. He knows God is leading him into a better future and will be with him along the way. But then, at the last minute, he decides not to go through with it.

What happened?

James was afraid. He knew his wife liked the security of his income, so he didn't even talk with her about his dream out of fear. So to play it safe at home, he pulled the plug on his plans. This put James in a downward spiral. He saw himself as weak and started questioning who he really was and what he should do next. Feeling depressed by betraying his core convictions, he reverted to some old bad habits to soothe himself, which only further weakened his identity.

Mike, on the other hand, took a different approach. Like James, he wanted to change his work situation and had his fears. But he refused to let fear stop him. He regularly meditated on his core convictions and believed God created him for a unique purpose. He also trusted that God would lead him through any challenges. With the help of his wife, Mike devised a plan for the transition. He is now working in an area that better uses his gifts and fulfills desires he's had for years. What's most satisfying for Mike is that he knows he is living in alignment with his core convictions and identity.

Make sure you understand the point of these two stories. As a man, you will aspire to live more in line with your identity. However, achieving this often comes with challenges. To overcome them, it's crucial to hold fast to your core convictions and trust God. Otherwise, you risk sabotaging yourself. Before moving forward, take a moment to reflect: "Is there any way I'm undermining my own goals?"

The role of the conscience
Your conscience plays an important part in navigating the challenges you face as a man. And paying attention to your conscience will not only help guide you, it will increase the strength of your identity. So continually calibrate your conscience to God's Word, and make following it the norm for you.

The life of the Apostle Paul offers profound insights into the relationship between conscience and identity. In the book of Acts, Paul mentions he made it his practice to keep a clear conscience before God and man (Acts 24:16). This is a curious statement, but it makes sense when you recall Paul had a history as a proud man who found his identity in his heritage, status, zeal and self-righteousness. When Paul saw the light and realized how misguided he was, he could have been weighed down by his conscience. But he wasn't. Having received the grace of God, he became a new man, and his conscience was cleared. And possessing a new identity, he moved on with the mission God had for him–always seeking to have a clear conscience before God and man. Through this approach, Paul not only maintained a strong identity, but persevered in his mission and changed the world.

This principle of keeping a good conscience before God and man is one we all should adopt. If your conscience is ever troubling you, ask God to show you why and respond accordingly. Be quick to change your mind, repent, and head in what you know is the right direction. This will bring you back in alignment with your core convictions, and help maintain the strength of your identity.

Ultimately, make a habit of living by the standards you say you believe. Your integrity, character and identity are all woven together.

ESSENTIAL ELEMENT #3: TELLING YOURSELF THE RIGHT STORY

We are storytelling people. We tell stories to others. People tell stories to us. And we tell stories to ourselves. None of this is surprising, since we are made in God's image and live in a world where He is unfolding His story. We are people with stories, all living within God's all-encompassing narrative.

The stories we adopt play a significant role in forming our identities because we can see ourselves identifying with a part in any story.

So be mindful of how you see yourself fitting into the stories you hear or tell.

Today, people tell or believe a variety of stories about themselves. And to the extent these stories deviate from the truth of God's story, they lead men away from their true identity.

Here are some of the most common stories men may adopt:

- **The Rugged Individualist Story**... "I can become whatever I want to be through my own self-reliance."

- **The Self-Made Man Story**..."I've become a success through my own efforts and on my own terms, and I'm proud of it.

- **The Victim Story**... "I've been oppressed and treated unfairly, so I'm at a disadvantage and entitled to...."

- **The 'My Life is Over' Story**... "I've made too many big mistakes to have any meaningful future. I'm hopelessly irredeemable.

- **The Family Heritage Story**... "My family has always... so I will always..."

- **The Labor Theory of Value Story**... "I have worked so hard so I am deserving."

- **The 'I'm a Rotten Person' Story**... "I've hurt a lot of people in my life so I expect nothing good from my own."

- **The 'Prove Them Wrong' Story**... "No one thinks I can do anything of value so I'm going to prove them otherwise."

- **The 'I'm an Oppressor' Story...** "I have some money and am a certain race, so I must be guilty of oppression.

- **The 'I'm Never Good Enough' Story...** "If I just keep going and try a little harder, then they'll see my worth and embrace me.

I'm sure you can identify with some of these stories. You may even be living in one or more of them now. There is truth to be found among these narratives. People have achieved through hard work, made mistakes that are hard to overcome, and been mistreated. But none of these provide the whole story, from God's perspective. And if you let them become your dominant narrative, your God-given identity will never fully form.

So how do we avoid adopting a false narrative and living in an unhelpful story? Especially when those around you or your culture may be pushing you into one? Here are a few pointers to guide you.

1. **Don't be taken captive by deception or lies** (Col. 2:8).
Be on guard against ideas that may seem compelling because they're currently in vogue, and beware of movements that burden people with false guilt. Keep renewing your mind–and your identity–with your core convictions.

2. **Don't let the past define you** (1 Cor. 6:11).
The devil will do all he can to accuse you regarding regrets from the past. But don't let his accusations stick. Through faith in Christ, you are forgiven, no longer under condemnation, and possess a new identity. And this allows you to enter into a new, better story.

3. **Don't forget God's grace** (Psalm 106).
We regularly forget the extent of God's kindness and the many ways He's delivered us. When this happens, our hearts grow cold with unbelief and we make choices that don't reflect our God-given identity. So keep remembering God's story of redemption, and how you are a part of it. He is not done delivering you.

As you apply these safeguards in your own life, they will help you reframe your story as a subplot of God's larger story for humanity. The world, the flesh and the devil constantly seek to frame a narrative for you that's driven by guilt, bitterness and pride. But you can escape this by re-framing your story in line with God's grand drama, where good conquers evil, and you humbly serve as a son, heir and co-ruler with Him.

The three elements I've related in this chapter are essential to forming and keeping a strong identity. Pay attention to them like the balance in your checking account. You need to know where you stand every day.

So:

- **Keep nurturing your core beliefs.**

- **Take your standards and habits seriously.**

- **And be careful of the narrative you are following.**

I'll have more specific ideas about how to do this in Chapter 10. For now, just commit to making these essential elements a priority.

Men are accustomed to tracking all kinds of areas of their lives, from fitness to finances. But nothing is more worthwhile than monitoring the three elements presented in this chapter. Where you stand with these will affect who you become as a man and eventually determine the impact of your life on the world.

Brief Self-Assessment

1. What are your core convictions?

2. Are you living consistently with these convictions? What changes do you need to make?

3. What story are you telling yourself? What story do you need to tell yourself?

Breakthrough Insight:
Staying grounded in your core convictions, living consistently with them, and seeing the story of your life within God's overall redemptive narrative is essential to growing strong in your God-given identity, as well as fulfilling His purpose for your life.

PART THREE

Living Out Your God-Given Identity

CHAPTER NINE

PUTTING OFF THE OLD IDENTITY AND PUTTING ON THE NEW

Welcome to the third and final section of this guide. In this part of the book we're going to focus on implementation. Specifically, we will look at what you need to do to effectively walk in your God-given identity. In this particular chapter, we're going to consider the necessity of breaking free from any hindrances of your past.

Our past has a powerful influence on how we view both ourselves and our prospects for the future. And our histories can have a grip on us for decades, holding us back from living out our true God-given identity. Breaking free from the past is possible, and many have done it. But this requires a genuine desire to change. No one stumbles into a new, stronger identity and the liberty that comes with it. You have to be intentional about embracing it. So it's fitting to start this chapter about implementation by asking: Do you want to change?

You may be thinking, "Of course I want to change, that's why I'm still reading!" This is good, but we need to note that real change calls for more than consuming content. People take in vast amounts of content these days yet they remain unchanged. That's because true transformation requires a faith that leads to action. And whether any of us end up doing what must be done comes down to our desires, and whether we really want to see a difference.

There's a story in the Gospel of John where Jesus comes upon a man who had been an invalid for thirty-eight years. Jesus asks the man, "Do you want to get well?" (Jn. 5). It seems like an unnecessary question, as we assume the man must want to get better. But can we know for sure? Maybe he's used to living as a paralytic and is comfortable finding his identity as one? So Jesus tests his desire by telling him, "Get up, pick up your mat and walk." And he did!

In a related way, we must allow the Spirit to search our own hearts and reveal whether we truly want to live according to our God-given identity. Each of us must consider, "Do I really want to change and get well?" This is a big question. Really big. How you answer will set the trajectory for the rest of your life and determine whether you live out God's intended purpose for you.

So what do you think? Are you ready for the change living in your God-given identity will bring? If so, the process is quite straightforward.

Putting Off the Old and Putting on the New
We can picture the change we must embrace as a matter of putting off the old and putting on the new. The Bible speaks of this specifically in reference to putting away certain behaviors and replacing them with new ones (Eph. 4:22ff.). So, for example, it tells us to lay aside falsehood and instead speak the truth, as a way of living consistently with the transforming power of the gospel. This same put off/put on principle also applies at the foundational level of our identity. And it points to the need for all who profess faith in Jesus to put off their old identity and put on the new one found in Him.

Staying with this imagery, envision the process of adopting your true identity like putting on a new coat. You go to the closet and instead of putting on your old jacket with the dirty cuffs and collar, you put on the new one there waiting for you every day. That's how simple it is to embrace your new identity, except for one difference. Rather than putting your arms through sleeves, you put your whole being into the hands of God by faith as one who belongs to Him.

Your flesh (or old man) will resist this, as it urges you to stick with the old way of viewing yourself and your old way of life. There are several reasons you may be tempted to go along with this. Let's examine these reasons so you understand what you must overcome to implement the truths of this guide.

The Love of Comfort
We humans enjoy our comfort, not just by way of cushy chairs, comfort foods, and predictable schedules, but also by maintaining a familiar self-image or identity. There's nothing wrong with comfort per se, unless your attachment to it is keeping you from entering the place God is calling you. So breaking from the comforts of the past, letting go of your old self, and getting adjusted to your God-given identity may be exactly what's needed to become all He intends you to be.

The Inclination to Conform
Most of us tend to conform to the culture, expectations, and pressures around us. We find it easier this way, and sometimes assume that being a 'good Christian' requires us to go with the flow. But this can prevent you from living out your true identity. For example, family pressure may stop you from following God in a direction different from the rest of the family. There's an expectation that you'll just stay as you've always been. And because of this pressure, many people settle for fitting in rather than breaking free from the mold. A friend of mine calls this being held back by 'love lines,' or the ties to those we love and care about.

The Lack of Conviction
Sometimes people won't take the step to embrace their God-given identity because they don't feel compelled about its importance. They may look at their lives and know some things should change, and realize they are falling short of what could be, but they decide they've been managing okay. And without the needed motivation, they become distracted, default to their old familiar priorities, and stay the same as they've always been–even though they know a change for the better is within reach.

These constraints are common, keeping countless people stuck in a less-than-ideal life. To escape this, it's important to realize that God truly has something more for you. And not only that, He wants to accomplish more through you.

Remember how we discussed that God designed you with a specific purpose in mind? For that purpose to be fulfilled, you need to see yourself as He does, because everything else flows from embracing who God created you to be.

This is why I'm taking the time to address these hindrances to actually implementing your God-given identity. Now, let's cover the biggest one of them all.

Shame
Shame has imprisoned more souls than all the tyrants in history combined. By shame, I refer to the pain and humiliation we feel when our conscience makes us aware of something wrong or foolish we've done. Shame can also arise if someone exposes an embarrassing truth about us or attributes a lie to us that reflects poorly on our character.

Humanity's acquaintance with shame goes back to the beginning. The Bible tells us that when Adam was created and living in his true identity, he was not ashamed. But after rejecting the identity God had for him and rebelling, he was stricken with shame, as evidenced by his attempt to hide from his Maker.

We can all identify with the powerful influence of shame when our conscience condemns us for our failures. The most damaging aspect is how shame can make us believe there is no escape from its dark shadow or possibility of new life, leading many to live without hope of change. This often results in idling away their days with destructive habits as a way of coping with their pain and atoning for their shame.

By its nature, shame is oppressive, holding multitudes back from venturing into the true identity and purpose God has for them. Shame is sticky too. It stays with you. And sadly, many people die in their shame.

But shame is not so sticky that you can't get rid of it. By God's grace, you can, because He has entered our world to deliver all who turn to Him in faith. In His mercy, He removes our transgressions from us as far as the east is from the west (Ps. 103:12), He lifts our heads and functions as a shield about us (Ps. 3:3), and positions us to experience a new life without condemnation (Rom. 8:1).

This reality is available no matter what your past experience or current condition.

The Apostle Paul makes this plain with his teaching and example. In his first letter to the Corinthians, Paul addresses former idolaters, fornicators, adulterers, homosexuals, thieves and drunkards, emphasizing that this was no longer their identity by stating "such *were* some of you" (1 Cor. 6:9-11). Paul could say this confidently because he had undergone a similar transformation, as he went from a proud persecutor of the church to a new man in Christ. This renewal allowed Paul to live without shame, with a clear self-awareness and a strong sense of mission. And His transformation not only changed his life but also impacted the world.

Because shame is so powerful, I encourage you to reflect on your own experience with shame and recognize how it may be hurting you. Is shame causing you to keep God and others at a distance? Is it keeping you stuck in misery and darkness? Or is it trapping you in a negative narrative about your past, present, and future? If so, you don't have to stay there. By humbly stepping into the light of God's grace, all this can change.

And all it takes is laying your guilt and shame before Christ, and putting on His righteousness by faith (2 Cor. 5:21). As you do, your identity is no longer tied to what you have done–or what has been done to you–but it's secured in the One who redeems and restores. And with this come plans for good, to give you a future and a hope (Jer. 29:11).

If you have been struggling with shame, now is the time to deal with it once and for all. It's essential to embracing your God-given identity and moving into the life God has for you. Simply come to Him and ask that He would restore you with a prayer like this one:

Almighty God and Merciful Father, I come to you as the sovereign Lord over all. I confess I have brought shame upon myself by choosing to go my own way. Forgive me of my sin, and cleanse me of all unrighteousness. Remove the shame that oppresses me every day. Through the righteousness of Christ, allow me to boldly fulfill the purpose you have for my life as I live out a new identity in Him. In His Name, Amen.

I urge you to deal with any shame or other obstacles that hinder you from putting on your new identity in Christ. Taking this step has major implications: it delivers you from a life of slavery and sets you on a path of freedom, productivity, and joy in God's kingdom.

Living in Freedom
To live with a false identity is to exist in a type of slavery, as you live by lies that keep you in bondage rather than in the truth God intends for you. To change this, you must both receive the deliverance God offers you AND walk in the truth of that deliverance in your daily life.

One of the best illustrations of this comes from the people of Israel and their experience coming out of Egypt. After 430 years, God delivered the Israelites from their Egyptian bondage. Not only that, He set them on a course to thrive in the Promised Land where they would enjoy liberty and prosperity. Yet this did not come easily for Israel. They were accustomed to seeing themselves as slaves, rather than people of God destined for freedom. And as a result, an entire generation of people failed to enter into the land God had promised and prepared for them.

Notice that Israel's deliverance from Egypt was just a starting point. To fully experience the freedom and life God had for them, they had to see themselves differently and take responsibility to make the most of the opportunity God put before them. Otherwise, it meant dying in the wilderness.

The same thing is true for us today. It's possible to be delivered from the penalty and power of sin, know God's forgiveness, yet not walk in freedom. This requires something more. It takes habitually putting off the old and putting on the new, as we make a break with the attachments and thinking of the past, and press into all God has for us in our new identity. Without this, we remain oppressed like Israel and die without entering into what God has for us.

Jesus's own words about freedom are helpful here, as He tells His disciples that if they abide in His Word, they shall know the truth and the truth will set them free (John 8:31-32). The freedom He speaks of is more than just freedom from guilt. It's the liberty that comes from knowing you really are His child, valued and cared for by the Father, and chosen to bear fruit with your life as a light to the world.

It's this kind of freedom that transforms lives. And not just individual lives, but families, communities, and nations too. When people know their God-given identity, it gives them hope, vision, and drive to do good they didn't have before. With these qualities, they are empowered to move ahead with confidence in God and an expectancy He is going to work great things in their midst.

You can experience this for yourself, as a son, joint-heir and conqueror in Him, while putting off the old identity and putting on the new as your perpetual practice.

Again, this is something you enter into and live in BY FAITH. As you believe...

... if anyone is in Christ, he is a new creature; the old things passed away; behold, new things have come (2 Cor. 5:17).

Overcoming in Crises and Hard Times
As we wrap up this chapter, I want to give extra encouragement to those who have experienced crises or hard times that have left a mark on their identity. Life-changing events like a major illness or accident, moral failure, divorce, or job loss can really take a toll on

how a man views himself. These experiences can crush his identity, leaving him feeling like a failure with no hope for the future.

If this kind of situation describes your own, I encourage you to embrace the opportunity to rebuild your life. Think of it this way... In all likelihood, you probably had some struggles with your identity *before* going through your life-changing event. Now, on the other side of the crisis, your old identity has been broken down, ready to be cleared away, so you can embrace a new identity from God and build upon that. This is not a far-fetched idea. I have walked with men through this process and seen their lives rebuilt, with the new foundation better than the old. Also, remember, God is a God of great reversals, who is in the business of resurrecting what seem like lost causes, so there is hope.

No matter what your current situation, embracing your God-given identity is essential. It's a must for walking in freedom from the past and stepping into the purpose God ordained for you from the beginning.

The possibility of a transformed existence is available to you. This is the truth, no matter who you are. But you must respond and act on what you know and understand.

To help you move forward, here are five questions to assess your readiness to implement the truth about your identity:

1. Do you acknowledge Jesus Christ as Lord over all?

2. Do you want to serve as a co-creator and co-ruler with Him in today's world?

3. Do you desire to live in alignment with His truth?

4. Do you want your life to bless the world?

5. Do you hope the blessing you bring will affect generations to come?

If you answered 'yes' to these questions, it's time to shed your old identity and embrace the new one offered by your Creator and Redeemer. Walk in your new identity by faith, growing in understanding each day, and marvel at the transformation the Spirit will progressively work in your life.

Breakthrough Insight:
Adopting your God-given identity requires a desire for change and breaking free from any hindrances from the past. This may be challenging, but as you move forward and receive what God has for you in faith, you will enter into His plans and purposes for your life.

CHAPTER TEN

LIVING OUT YOUR IDENTITY IN EVERYDAY LIFE

For I am confident of this very thing, that He who began a good work in you will perfect it... (Philippians 1:6).

Living in keeping with your God-given identity will transform your life. This is due to a very simple principle:

If you know who you are, you will know what to do. But if you don't know who you are, you'll always be at a loss.

Put another way, ignorance of your true identity breeds confusion, uncertainty, and fear, which in turn fosters hesitancy. But knowing who you are brings clarity, vision, and courage, providing the confidence to move forward.

Living in your God-given identity leads to a completely changed life, as it equips you to live with assurance before God and others as a man. To embody this identity in your everyday life, there are a couple of aspects to keep in mind.

Two Dimensions of Your God-Given Identity to Remember
Think carefully about this... Your identity has both a definite and progressive aspect to it. The **definite** aspect refers to the objective reality of who you are as God sees you. It is a permanent feature of

your personhood, by virtue of being made in God's image and renewed by His grace through faith in His Son. Because this aspect of your identity is established by God, it is settled and unchanging. It is definite. It does not depend on how you feel or even how strong your faith is on any given day. It is secure in being a child of God who bears His likeness.

Yet there is a second aspect of your identity that is **progressive**. We call it progressive because it involves growing stronger in your identity over time as you deepen in understanding and faith. The significance of this is that the stronger you become in your identity, the more consistently you will live with it–and the more you will fulfill your potential as a special creation of God. Embracing this growing process is extremely important. Practically, it means holding on to the definite aspect of your identity as you are advancing in the progressive aspect, becoming increasingly aware of who you truly are in the Lord.

Let me illustrate this for you.

Living Without Fear
Imagine you have a fear of speaking up to address things you view as wrong. This might occur in your family, at work, socially, or in your community. You see things you know aren't right, and you'd like to say something about them, but you see yourself as unfit for the task, and out of fear you remain silent. After situations like this happen, you beat yourself up for not saying anything. Which only increases your struggles with how you view yourself.

But let's say a situation comes up and this time you are self-aware of your definite, God-given identity. So instead of going along with the old you, saying to yourself, "Oh, who am I to speak up? What do I know? I'll probably look foolish," you think, "Hey, I really need to say something and there's no reason I shouldn't. Sure, I don't know everything and I'm not perfect, but with my identity in Christ I have a role to play, and I can trust Him to lead me through whatever may come, so I'm going to speak up."

Do you see the difference that holding onto your identity while growing in it can make?

What I describe here applies to anything you may fear, whether it's fear of failure, worries over potential losses, anxiety about the unknown–you name it. Living in your God-given identity equips you to overcome any kind of fear or inhibition *because your confidence is ultimately in Him*. So it absolutely makes sense to stay mindful of your true identity as much as you can!

Now, since aligning yourself with your God-given identity is essential to functioning as God designed you, it's natural to wonder, "What can I do to hasten the growth of my identity?" A good place to start is by fixing your sights on Jesus.

Jesus, the Gold-Standard of Functioning in One's Identity
Jesus functioned in perfect keeping with His identity. He knew He was God's "beloved Son" from all eternity. Also, the relationship Jesus had with His Father was marked by oneness, instead of interrupted by sin as it is with us. And since this was forever the case for Him, He was completely secure in who He was.

Out of this strong identity, Jesus was well-equipped to fearlessly fulfill His earthly mission in union with His Father. This mission was demanding too. It involved: humbling Himself to take on human flesh, teaching the masses, ministering to outcasts, confronting hypocritical leaders, and ultimately giving up His life on a Roman cross.

I hope you see from Jesus what kind of power living in your true identity can bring. This is significant, because by faith we too are sons of the Father. And out of this identity we are able to carry out our own unique callings with the kind of fearlessness and trust Jesus demonstrated.

The only difference we must reckon with is this: for Jesus, there was never a gap between His identity and how He lived–ever. For us, there is. We all carry the baggage of sinful desires and wayward histories, making it easy to revert to our old ingrained identity and self-image.

But here's the good news: We can bridge the gap between who we really are in Christ and the actions that do not align with His character, enabling us to live more consistently with our true identity. All it requires is walking in trust with God the Father. As we become more accustomed to seeing ourselves as beloved sons of the Father—knowing that He loves us, cares for us, and is always working for our good—we're able to confidently pursue the life He intends for us, no matter where He may lead us.

Closing the gap between our true identity and how we conduct our lives is a process that requires self-awareness, learning, and time. But we can take part in moving this maturing process along by applying a number of practices.

Key Practices for Growing in Your God-Given Identity
The practices I mention here are traditionally known as 'means of grace" in Christian circles, because they are the 'means' by which God ordinarily gives us the grace we need to grow. As we are faithful with these practices, we become more and more oriented to the Father and stronger in our identity as His sons. So consider how you can best incorporate them in your life.

Reading and Listening to Scripture
Reading and listening to Scripture is essential for our spiritual nourishment. Jesus said, "Man cannot live by bread alone, but by every word that proceeds out of the mouth of God" (Mt. 4:4). With these words, Jesus highlighted the need we have for constant renewal in the way we think about ourselves and our place in God's world. There are many excellent programs available to guide you through reading the Bible. Additionally, I recommend listening to God's Word. Scripture itself tells us that faith comes by hearing, and with the abundance of Bible apps available, listening to Scripture is easily accessible. Immersing yourself in the Bible daily will refine your identity in the Lord, just as flowing water polishes a stone.

Tip: Come up with a plan to consume God's word daily that works well for you. Early in the day works best for most.

Meditation and Prayer
Meditation and prayer are great companions for functioning in your God-given identity. When people hear about meditating, they often think of emptying the mind of any thoughts. But biblical meditation involves taking the truths of God and pondering them from different angles. When you meditate on verses having to do with your identity, it bolsters your sense of who you are before God.

For example, try meditating on this verse and see if it deepens your sense of identity: "He chose us in Him before the foundation of the world, that we should be holy and blameless before Him in love" (Eph. 1:4). This truth clearly shows how intentional God has been regarding His purpose for you. Other identity verses to meditate on are available in the application guide.

Prayer is the way we communicate with God and personally engage our Father in heaven. It is how we do life with Him as we plan, encounter circumstances, seek help, and carry out His purpose for us. Beyond this, prayer helps us better see ourselves as the sons, heirs, and conquerors He has made us through Christ.

Tip: Be intentional about your prayer and meditation time. Without planning, it's all too easy for these moments to slip away.

Worship
Both private and corporate worship are vital for functioning in your God-given identity. Private worship can take place anywhere and anytime as a way to realign your life with God. Regarding corporate worship, I'm thinking mainly of the regular meeting of God's people on the Lord's Day. In this meeting, God takes the initiative to renew us by calling us into His presence, forgiving our sins, directing us through His Word, feeding us at His table, and recommissioning us in His service. In this way, God redirects us to Himself, providing necessary renewal for our souls–and identity–each week.

Tip: Make worship a non-negotiable part of your week.

Living in Community
Men often tend to isolate themselves and navigate life alone. But this approach does not foster a robust identity. Isolation can lead men to become overly introspective, fixating on questions about the meaning of their lives without finding positive resolutions. The antidote to this is for men to engage with a community of like-minded individuals, such as a church group or a dedicated group of men. Strengthening one's identity doesn't come from introspection; it's through regular interaction with a supportive band of brothers that men can best discern who they are and their role in the world.

Tip: Consider joining or starting a men's group at your church. It's a great way to build relationships with like-minded individuals and explore shared values and experiences.

Obeying what you know
It is well known that experience enhances understanding, and this principle extends to comprehending your God-given identity. If you habitually function independently of God, you will miss valuable experiences that contribute to understanding your identity from a divine perspective. But, if you cultivate a habit of following the Father's lead with the eagerness of a child ready to obey, you will gain a deeper grasp of who you are in the Lord. As the Bible puts it, "A good understanding have all those who do His commandments" (Psalm 111:10).

So if you want to perceive your God-given identity as fully as possible, make obeying Him something you will not compromise.

Tip: Keep a journal or notebook to record what God shows you as you obey him, especially in hard circumstances.

Implementing these practices will help you recognize your true identity and live it out. If incorporating them into your routine seems overwhelming, there's no need to feel anxious. Start where you are and progress step by step. You may already engage in some of these practices. If not, choose one or two to implement. With time and consistency, you'll find these practices becoming a natural part of your life, especially as they strengthen your sense of God-given identity.

Putting Your Identity to the Test
When it comes right down to it, you will grow most in your God-given identity as you put it to the test in your everyday life. This is

really a matter of reframing. To reframe something is to come at a situation or problem from a different perspective than you're used to. Reframing can help change your attitudes, beliefs and behaviors in all kinds of circumstances, as it brings a new way of understanding old issues.

Let's look at some examples where you can test your identity and use reframing to your advantage. As we explore these instances, pay close attention to the significant role your identity plays in each scenario.

Private life
We all face private battles that bring us face to face with various temptations. In our flesh–or old identity–we're accustomed to facing these battles in a particular way. Operating in the flesh does not deliver a great track record for any of us. But what if you were to start looking at your battles differently, from the perspective of your new identity in Christ? Think of a temptation you've often succumbed to. It may seem like this has become so much a part of who you are that it will always defeat you. Yet as you approach this in your new identity, you can frame the situation differently, seeing yourself as a new man with new priorities and power. And by the grace of God, you can overcome what's been ensnaring you.

Family
Family dynamics can often hinder us from fully embracing our true identity. As mentioned earlier, family expectations can exert pressure, conditioning us to fit certain roles or behave in specific ways. Alongside these external pressures, guilt—whether real or perceived—regarding parents, wife, or children can weigh heavily on a man. In such situations, it is crucial for a man to function within his God-given identity, discerning what faithfulness requires of him. This may involve seeking forgiveness for past offenses or

responsibly shouldering leadership burdens. Regardless, remaining rooted in his identity will fortify him to stay strong and make wise decisions.

Work

Any man can face setbacks in his vocational journey. How he responds is heavily influenced by his sense of identity. If his identity hinges on his performance, any rough day can sour his mood as he questions his worth and security. The antidote to this volatility is for a man to anchor his identity in the Lord. By doing so, he remains steady—neither overly elated when things go well nor despondent when they do not. This stability isn't a sign of apathy but steadfast trust in God, as he stays focused on using his unique gifts to serve others amidst daily opportunities. It's from this foundation of strong identity that a man not only handles daily ups and downs, but also makes meaningful contributions over the course of his career, adapting to the changes that come with time.

Church

Men often feel inferior in their relationship to the church, frequently due to assumptions they make about other men. They may believe that others have it all together while they do not. When men persist with this assumption, they're unlikely to get involved. To overcome this, it's essential to reframe the situation realistically, remembering that everyone in any church has issues. So there's no reason for any man to feel inferior; he is simply different. The best approach is for a man to walk humbly in his God-given identity and, from that foundation, encourage and build up others through his unique gifts. By doing so, he can contribute meaningfully to the church community and grow in his faith alongside others.

Society

Another area where men often need to reframe their thinking has to do with their role in society. Due to prevalent negative attitudes toward men, it's not unusual for many men to feel unwelcome in their own culture. This can lead them to retreat from the world and isolate themselves in their own interests. It's hard to blame men for such a response. But it is precisely in such an environment that we need men—not to give up, but to rise up and contend for what is true, right, and good. The only way men can do this effectively is by securing their identity in the Lord, rather than allowing it to be diminished by the world.

These are just a few examples of how a man can reframe everyday situations and approach them in greater accord with his God-given identity. There are countless other specific scenarios we could discuss, and I encourage you to think of some challenges you are currently facing that would benefit from a fresh perspective.

The central idea is this: remember who you are in your God-given identity. By staying conscious of who you are, you will be equipped to manage whatever challenges you encounter with faith, courage, and strength.

Making this a way of life may take time. You will encounter situations that tempt you to revert to your old identity. It's understandable to feel discouraged and consider returning to familiar ways. But remember, this is a process, and God will give you many opportunities to work out in your life what He is working on in your heart.

The Lord wants you living in your new identity in the context of your everyday life. It's why He has drawn you to Himself, and it's how He intends to accomplish His purpose through you. Be assured,

He will give you all the grace you need to live in your true identity as you seek Him and walk in the ways He leads you.

In this process, cling to the undeniable truth of who you are in the Lord. Never lose sight of the sonship and inheritance that are yours in Christ. Embrace the growing, progressive aspect of your identity, and rejoice in seeing the Spirit mature you and prepare you to fulfill the purpose He has for you.

There are great rewards for walking in your God-given identity, both for yourself and for those you have the opportunity to bless. So stay committed to this journey. As you do, you will become more aware of who God has made you to be and increasingly operate from that identity in your everyday life.

Breakthrough Insight:
There is a fixed, permanent part of your identity and there is a changing, growing part of your identity. The latter will develop best when you remember the former as you face the issues of your life.

CHAPTER ELEVEN

MOVING INTO YOUR GOD-GIVEN PURPOSE

This chapter serves as the culmination of the book. One might say it's the most important, as it brings together your identity and purpose.

It's crucial to understand that finding your identity is not the final goal but a means to fulfill God's intent for your life. Our identities form the foundation of who we are and act as a bridge to our purpose. If you're unsure of your identity, your true purpose will remain unclear. But once you are clear on your identity, your purpose will emerge, and you'll be ready to consciously carry out God's intent for your life.

So your identity is not like a trophy or figurine sitting on the shelf in your living room. It's functional. And God equips you with it to propel you forward as a man–self-aware of who you are and why you exist.

We've touched on the link between identity and purpose earlier in the book. But now it's time to develop the connection further and equip you with tools to move confidently into your purpose based on your identity. Let's begin by tackling a fairly common but challenging question.

How does a man find his purpose?
Imagine a friend reaches out to you at the end of the day and he's upset. His problem? He doesn't see the point of his life. He goes to work, has a little fun on weekends, and then does it all over again. It seems pointless to him. So he's hungry to find meaning, and he's looking to you for help. How would you answer him?

I would start by going back to the beginning, in the book of Genesis. There, God reveals two essential truths for every person: (1) He created us in His image (Gen. 1:26) and (2) He made us for dominion (Gen. 1:28). In these truths, every man finds the foundation he needs to discover both his identity and purpose, which are closely connected.

We can understand the connection between identity and purpose by recalling the familiar "form follows function" principle used by designers and architects. The essence of this principle is that the design of something is determined by its use or purpose. For example, a home, a gym, and an office building will each have different designs because their functional needs dictate their overall layout and structure.

In a similar way, God created us in a specific form for a particular function. From the beginning, it has been His plan to craft beings who would join Him in the glorious work of developing and ruling the earth. So He fashioned us in His likeness to make this possible. In other words, He has given us our identity as His image-bearers so we can fulfill the purpose of functioning as His partners and co-laborers in the work of dominion.

This applies to every human being who has ever lived. So if you are a man seeking to find your own purpose, this is where to begin. Embrace the identity God has designed for you, and from there, enter into the common purpose He has given you along with the rest of humanity.

Your Purpose in General
We can get an idea of what functioning in your purpose looks like in general by recalling the way God charged Adam to cultivate and keep the Garden of Eden (Gen. 2:15). With this commission, Adam received the responsibility of both developing and protecting the garden. This responsibility also included God's basic command to "be fruitful and multiply" (Gen. 1:28).

We've already considered how this directive applies to all humanity, but what I'd like to highlight here is how every man carries with him the call to both develop and protect whatever God entrusts to his care.

We see this in the Bible when Nehemiah was busy rebuilding the walls of Jerusalem. As Nehemiah worked, he had a sword in one hand and a trowel in the other, demonstrating the simultaneous need to build something up while protecting it from harm. This principle applies to our own day as well. Consider our homes: we put a welcome mat on the porch to foster community and a lock on the door to provide protection.

What's important to note is how this call to develop and protect is part of every man's general purpose–including your own. And it's a worthwhile exercise to consider the different ways you already put this into practice in the different domains of your own life, from your family, to your work, and your community.

I should mention too, this inclination to develop and protect is wired into a man's being and exists throughout his life. While recently talking with a widow in our neighborhood, she told me some of her husband's last words were, "Don't forget to lock the doors at night," which was his way of expressing his protective purpose until the very end of his life.

Every man is created with this same instinct to develop and protect. It may not always function as it should, but it is there.

> **Pause to Apply:** What are some ways you see your inclination to develop and protect in the different domains of your life?

Your Particular Purpose
In addition to the general purpose God has given every man to be fruitful with his life, He also provides each one with a specific reason for living. Consider this: the Lord has placed you in a distinct time and place, within a particular family with its own history and characteristics. He has also endowed you with individual gifts and interests that shape who you are. Together, these fill out your identity. And it's from this unique identity you are in a one-of-a-kind position to serve your world.

The service a man brings commonly happens within his vocation, but it is not limited to that. You can also fulfill your individual purpose as a volunteer, while pursuing your interests, through your family, and in the way you engage people every day.

Paying attention to your interests is crucial for identifying your unique purpose and understanding how to best use your gifts. For example, I've always been intrigued by words and writing. I remember receiving a vocabulary calendar as a Christmas gift in junior high—it was one of my most memorable presents. I also recall eagerly poring over the bullet points of a monthly newsletter my dad received. And I remember how much I enjoyed writing a weekly newspaper column. Over time, writing has become a core part of who I am and a primary way I fulfill my purpose in the world.

Your interests and experience can help to guide you as well. You have unique factors that make up who you are. As they all come together, they not only define your identity but also help indicate what you should do. And really, anything is possible. I know of someone who saw himself as a 'skateboarder for Jesus.' This may sound crazy, but as he lived this out, God used him in the lives of others in remarkable ways. This example illustrates the extent to which God can take the gifts, interests and background of any one of us to use for His purposes.

Another thing to keep in mind as you consider your unique purpose is this: No one can fulfill the place you're in like you can–at least at this moment. That's likely why God has you there! So, be careful of assuming God wants you somewhere else. He may, but give thought to how you can bring your gifts to bear on the opportunities He is giving you where He has you now.

Pause to Apply: How do you see your gifts and interests playing a part in the particular purpose God has for you?

Functioning in Your Identity and Purpose

Once you have a good sense of your identity–i.e. know who you are–it's time to build upon it and move forward. But how do you advance? I believe these three elements are essential for moving from your identity into your purpose.

Calling
Number one is calling. People often assume there is a lot of mystery behind the concept of calling, and with this comes the assumption that one's calling is hard to perceive. My own conviction is that finding your calling usually isn't as difficult as it's made out to be. Simply put, I believe a calling occurs when a man's desires and abilities intersect with an issue or problem he can solve.

Take Roger, for example. He became aware of poor water quality in his town and felt a strong desire to address this issue for the good of the community. Drawing on his training as a civil engineer and experience with public health issues, Roger realized he was uniquely positioned to help. This conviction led him to sense a calling to take action and resolve the problem, no matter the challenges he would face.

Overall, the concept of calling is as simple as this. So, as you build upon your identity and move forward in it, I encourage you to consider a few questions: What are the things you enjoy doing? What are some activities people have acknowledged you excel in? And how might you use your gifts and abilities to serve others and address needs around you?

Vision
The second element you need to move forward in your purpose is vision. This, too, may seem like an esoteric topic, but I believe it also is more straightforward than we tend to realize. God made us to think in pictures. So when we contemplate how He may be calling us to a specific role or action, we can envision what fulfilling that calling might look like. These images often reveal actionable steps. When you consider the entirety of what you see, you possess what we call vision–to inspire and direct you in the way ahead.

If you believe God is calling you in a certain direction but lack accompanying vision, it could mean a couple of things. It might indicate that He's not calling you in the way you initially assumed, as callings typically come with some form of accompanying vision. Alternatively, a lack of vision may suggest the need for more prayer, asking God to reveal what you need to see.

Faith

Once God gives you vision, the time comes when you must take action. Otherwise, all you're left with is an idea or dream. Taking action requires faith, which the Bible describes as the assurance of things hoped for and the conviction of things not seen (Heb. 11:1). Faith enables us to act on possibilities that we envision but have not yet materialized. To act on faith, we must step forward believing God will lead us, provide for us, and bless us for faithfully responding to His guidance.

Each of these elements–calling, vision, and faith–work together to move you from your God-given identity into the purpose He has for you. Because these elements are so vital to you living in your purpose, it makes sense for you to get familiar with them and recognize how they may be at work in your own heart in any situation.

Pause to Apply: Do you perceive any particular calling at present? Do you have a vision of what responding to that call might look like? And do you have the faith to proceed?

When You're Afraid of Big Moves

It's not uncommon for anxiety or fear to overshadow us when contemplating significant decisions or changes, so let's explore this challenge further. The main issue with fear isn't merely its discomfort, but its tendency to immobilize us and keep us from fully entering into God's plans. Yet once we overcome fear, we're able to enter the unknown, confront difficulties, and pursue paths that might seem risky to others.

The Bible, of course, offers abundant wisdom on fear, and the comforting command to 'fear not' is a familiar one. We can assume Scripture tells us not to be afraid for our emotional support, but the bigger reason it exhorts us this way is so we'd carry out the purpose God has for us. In other words, God tells us not to fear so we would be faithful to fulfill whatever mission He entrusts to us. Consider, for instance, how God told Joshua, Gideon, the Israelites, Mary and the disciples not to fear–so they would fulfill the unique missions He had for each of them.

Take to heart the Bible's call to live fearlessly as you consider what God may be calling you to do. Moving forward in His purpose takes faith and, at times, bravery, especially in today's culture, which is resistant to biblical values and places a strong emphasis on safety. These factors can discourage us from taking the risks that answering God's call may require. So it's essential to know how to confront your fears. The best approach is to constantly remember your identity as a child of the Father and live by faith in His ongoing care.

Remembering Your God-Given Identity
So as you think about stepping into the purpose God has for you, stay mindful of the identity He has graciously provided you. This awareness will give you the security you need to move faithfully in the direction God leads you. It will also provide the strength, grace and wisdom you must have to implement His purpose for you day by day.

Remember this truth about yourself... As an image-bearer of God, He designed you for dominion and a fruitful existence. You are made to multiply, develop and protect in the different domains of life He sets before you. God has created you for such things, and He has granted you the authority to carry them out. So do them with confidence!

Remember that through faith in Christ, you have a new relationship with God. You are no longer an enemy under condemnation but have been made His child, a friend, co-laborer, and heir of His kingdom by grace. This new relationship assures you of God's unwavering commitment. He will never leave you nor forsake you. With this understanding, you can respond faithfully and follow Him wherever He leads.

Finally, remember that you are not left to your own resources to fulfill God's purpose for your life. You are a new creation. It is no longer you who lives, but Christ who lives in you (Gal. 2:20). And He is constantly at work within you to accomplish His will. God is your source for all things–direction, power, hope, wisdom, even faith itself–through his Spirit. So keep turning to Him to live out the purpose He has for you.

Remember, remember, remember these truths!

Tip: Hide this verse in your heart – ""For it is God who works in you to will and to act in order to fulfill His good purpose" (Phil. 2:13).

Staying Proactive in Your Identity and Purpose
As we approach the end of this guide, I encourage you to stay proactive when it comes to your identity and purpose. This will

assure that you keep progressing. Be aware that we all can function in one of three ways–passively, reactively, or proactively.

By default, we often become passive, accepting what comes our way without actively responding or resisting. If you are passive about your identity and purpose, you will revert to old habits and ways of thinking under the pressure of current trends or personal situations. So avoid letting yourself function in a passive mode.

We can also operate reactively. When we're reactive, we only respond to events after they occur, rather than taking initiative. This approach lacks foresight and planning, and ends up hindering you from growing in your identity and purpose. Make it a habit to avoid functioning reactively as much as possible.

The most effective way to function is proactively. When you are proactive, you make plans and set goals that align with God's purpose and vision for you. Under the Spirit's guidance, being proactive gives you the insight to anticipate future events and needs. And consistently maintaining a proactive approach positions you to fulfill God's purpose in every area of your life.

Take note, staying proactive doesn't mean constantly being in motion. Being proactive can sometimes appear passive, like when you're exercising patience. But being proactive does mean staying engaged, with one eye to the God who made you and another to what He has called you to do.

Tip: Consider what steps you can take to proactively strengthen your identity and better carry out your purpose. Don't hesitate to review sections of this book for help.

God intends your life to have an effect, to bring good to your world. You can pursue this with confidence because He's given you a secure identity and a purpose that matters.

Breakthrough Insight:

Every man has a mandate to cultivate and protect his portion of the world with God. He also has a specific purpose that only he can fulfill. This includes you.

CONCLUSION

WHAT TO DO NEXT

We've reached the end of this guide. I hope it has helped you consider truths about your identity—and ultimately your life's purpose—at a level you haven't before. I also pray that what you've read here will inspire you as you seek to make your unique contribution to the world.

As we conclude this journey, it's worth noting that many popular stories feature characters who rise to do good after discovering their true identity. We see this theme in *The Chronicles of Narnia*, *The Lord of the Rings*, *Harry Potter*, *The Lion King*, and many others.

These stories captivate and inspire us because they resonate with our desires to understand who we are, live a purposeful life, and embark on adventures. Pursuing such a life is a noble goal, and this book aims to help you uncover your role in God's grand unfolding story–the narrative of His creation, the fall of mankind, and the redemption of all things through Jesus Christ.

To recap, here are some highlights of what we've covered in the book:

1. In the first few chapters we saw how there is definitely hope for men to discover and become solid in the identity God has for them.

We also considered why it's critical for men to become established in their identity, and discussed some of the main obstacles men face in accomplishing this today.

2. Next, we looked at the key for any man to come to know his identity, and how embracing his identity is a relatively simple process.

We also considered why men can still find adopting their true identity difficult.

3. In the next section, we explored the foundation of your identity, and why this is fundamental to your whole approach to life.

In exploring this, we unpacked a biblical framework for living, as well as the essential elements for growing and staying strong in your identity.

4. Then we focused on implementation, beginning with putting off your old identity and putting on the new.

From there, we considered living out your God-given identity in everyday life, including illustrations of what this looks like and ways it can transform how you address ordinary circumstances.

5. Finally, we looked at the important connection between your identity and your purpose.

Here we were able to see not just how living in your true identity supplies your life with meaning, but serves as the basis for fulfilling your unique purpose in the world God has made.

Now, you may be wondering where to go from here.

What To Do Next

The answer is to start regularly applying the principles from this book. We've covered the essentials you need to move from where you are today to becoming secure in your God-given identity.

If you would like additional help with this, check out the course I've created on this subject.

The course dives deeper and from different angles, providing additional teaching, application questions, and bonus content.

You can find more information about the course here:
madefordominion.com/identity-book-extras/

My goal is to help you gain a strong understanding of who you are and what God desires for your life. Everything I create is designed to support you in fulfilling your place in His kingdom.

David Bostrom

ADDITIONAL RESOURCES

The Identity Advantage: Application Guide
This is a free workbook to help you engage the material in the book.

Made for Dominion Daily
Each weekday I send out an email to encourage men seeking to live faithfully in their God-given identity and purpose in every area of life.

Get Dominion **book**
This book is an excellent companion to *The Identity Advantage,* as it expands on the topic of purpose discussed in this book.

Discovering Your God-Given Identity Course
This course goes in greater depth on the subject of identity. Its goal is to help those who go through it become thoroughly-grounded in their identity.

Access these resources by visiting:

madefordominion.com/identity-book-extras/

ABOUT THE AUTHOR

David Bostrom has been encouraging and equipping men for more than three decades. He served as a pastor for over twenty years and is currently the director of Made for Dominion Ministries.

David believes helping men recover their God-given identity and purpose is essential to renewing families, churches, communities and society as a whole.

When David is not helping men, he enjoys taking in Florida's natural wonders, staying physically active, and grilling for his family.

He is married and has six sons.

Made in United States
Orlando, FL
22 December 2024